Freakishly Effective
Social Media
for Network Marketing

D0061553

RAY HIGDON & JESSICA HIGDON

Published by
Success in 100 Pages
www.SuccessIn100Pages.com

ISBN 978-1-947814-98-1

Copyright © March 2018

All rights reserved.

LEGAL DISCLAIMER:

●●●

SPECIAL OFFER:

Grab Ray & Jessica Higdon's Brand New "Social Networker Series" on Video for 93% OFF!

Learn:

- How to Set up Your Social Media Profile the Right Way for MAXIMUM Results

- Exactly What to Post to Attract Perfect Customers and Biz Builders to You

- What to say Word-for-Word to People on Social Media Even if You Don't Know Them

- Scripts on What to Say to Get People to Join or Enroll

- Step-by-Step How to Build Locally Using Social Media!

Get Access to ALL FIVE Offers for the

LOW PRICE of ONLY $7.

(That's 93% Off!)

at www.SocialNetworkerSeries.com

●●●

FOREWORD BY
KIM GARST

It will come as no surprise to you that marketing has changed significantly over the past decade. If you've spent any time at all on Facebook, Instagram or Twitter, you'll have seen many different strategies and tactics being used – some extremely effective ones and others, well, not so much.

You've probably also seen many network marketing professionals using social media to attract prospects and build their teams. Again, you've likely seen some of these businesses *killing it* on social media – while others post every single day, but don't seem to be gaining any traction.

So, what's the difference between the network marketing professionals who are killing it on social media and those who aren't?

Ray hit my radar several years ago via a live video he was doing. His knowledge and passion for both people who are involved in network marketing and social media were immediately apparent to me. It was also immediately apparent that Ray was among the network marketing professionals who knew *exactly* how to use social media to build his business – all while remaining authentic, heart-centered and passionate about the people he served. That won me over immediately!

Since that time, I've had the opportunity to work with Ray in a number of different settings, including when he hired me for a VIP day, and later as a speaker at one of his live events. I've been consistently impressed with Ray's integrity and how much he cares about making an impact and a difference in people's lives.

His new book, *Freakishly Effective Social Media for Network Marketing*, is his latest offering to network marketing professionals who want to use social media to explode their businesses, all while maintaining their authenticity and integrity.

As Ray and Jessica acknowledge, there are plenty of books out there that will show you how to use social media for your business. However, this book isn't just a generic social media "how to" guide; it's a concise, value-packed, step-by-step guide to using social media to authentically build your *network marketing business*.

From which social media platforms to use, to identifying your target audience, to what types of content you should post – it's all in this book. Ray and Jessica also delve deeper, into how to establish authentic connections with your prospects...instead of annoying or alienating them.

Over the past few years, you may have noticed that live video on social media has exploded. Businesses are using live video on Facebook and Instagram, as well as on live streaming apps like Periscope, to reach their audience in new and exciting ways. However, knowing *how* to use live video is still a challenge for many marketers.

Ray and Jessica offer some great tips for how to use live video for your networking marketing business – including how to find topics for your videos, which platforms to use, and one of my favorite parts of the book, *The Freakishly Effective Four-*

Step Video Formula.

Whether you've been using social media for your network marketing business for a while, or are just getting your feet wet, you're sure to find valuable, actionable tips within the pages of this book.

It's a must read for anyone who wants to build their network marketing business on social media strategically, effectively, and with integrity!

Kim Garst

International Best-Selling Author of "Will The Real You Please Stand Up: Show Up, Be Authentic and Prosper in Social Media", and Forbes Top 10 Social Media "Power Influencer"

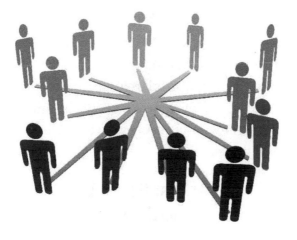

Introduction:

Before we placed our fingers on the keyboard and typed the first words of this manuscript, there were several things we wanted to be clear about. The first is: *Why should we write this book?* After all, it's not like there is a shortage of books on social media out there.

So to get that clarity, we did what we always do when deciding if we should launch a new product or service in our business. We dug deeper, asking the most important question: *What are the intended outcomes of the book—for you, the reader, and for the network marketing profession overall?*

The Purpose of This Book

The purpose of this book is not to try and convince you that you should be using social media to grow your business. You already know that, right? Nor is it to dig into the *technical aspects* of setting up your accounts, profiles, etc. There are thousands of resources available for doing that online already.

Quite simply, our goal for this book is to change the way people in the network marketing profession utilize what is undeniably the most powerful recruiting and marketing tool invented in the history of the world. We also aim to do it in a way that accelerates your success while elevating network marketing as a profession.

How Most People Use Social Media

Most people in network marketing look at social media as if it were a dartboard you can just throw things at, and that something will hit the mark—success will happen. They *hope* someone will respond. They *hope* someone will buy. They *hope* their business will grow. But *hope is not an effective marketing strategy.*

And so that's the big problem with treating social media like a dartboard. Most of the darts end up missing the mark. You *think* you're making progress, that you're getting traction in the marketplace—but you aren't.

There's good news, though, because there's a better approach. An approach that works. An approach that works *freakishly well.* Assuming...

Assuming you use social media the right way—the way we suggest on the following pages. Otherwise, quite frankly, you'd be better off binge-watching the new season of *Game of Thrones.*

About Us...

For those of you who don't know us, we want to share a little background about who we are and how we got here, to this place and time—writing these words for you.

Ray's Story...

I found network marketing through a real estate partner of mine. It was February 2006 and a juice product was on my mind.

That's right. It was a juice product, and I ended up getting it for my Mom as a gift, then found myself bit by the network marketing bug. After looking at the business model and really studying it, I knew it was a good option for me. But I also didn't know the first thing about network marketing, so I did just about everything wrong. Fast-forward 11 companies over a three-year period—I never had a major success.

During that same time, the real estate market crashed. I lost a lot of money and a lot of properties. Next thing I knew, I was in personal foreclosure and being chased by bill collectors.

On July 15, 2009, I had a new vision. Sick and tired of being a victim, I got truly serious about network marketing. I worked relentlessly and prospected like crazy. In fact, that was the period when I was going for 20 "no's," a day, working day and night. It worked for a while. I quickly became the number-one earner in that company.

Simultaneously, I dove into learning internet marketing because that was where a lot of business was being done. I began marketing online, teaching people what I knew and what worked and what didn't work. I realized everything you can do offline in network marketing, you can do online. And so that became an important part of how I grew my business.

At the same time, Jessica was proving that to be true, too, building her business online using social media. Little did I know at that time what Jessica and I would build together.

Jessica's Story...

When I first entered into social media, I was already committed to 90 hours a week of school and work, so time was a precious asset—so precious, in fact, I had roughly 30 minutes a day to build my business. I was 21 years old, with no options when it came to my warm market of friends and family.

I needed to find a different way to build my home business. The solution had to extend beyond my warm market, generate more leads, and do all this efficiently. That's when I learned there were people successfully building online businesses using social media.

I asked myself: *"If they can do it, why can't I?"*

After a lot of trial, error and tribulation, I finally found a strategy that worked. Not only did it work for me in my quest to build product sales, it worked in terms of finding business builders. I went from not signing up anyone in my business for the previous six months to having my first $10k month...*in less than 18 months*!

After that, I went on to become the number-one female income earner with that company. And 95% of my success was done through social media.

Within just a few years people from different companies and teams started asking me, *"How are you building your business online?"* At the same time, my husband, Ray, was teaching people all the strategies that got *him* to the number-one spot within *his* network marketing company. We decided it was time to build a company where, together, we could make a massive impact.

We launched our network marketing training company, and it has grown like mad. Today, The Higdon Group is one of *Inc. Magazine's* 5,000 fastest growing companies, having been featured in places like Inc.com, Huffingtonpost.com, and many other publications. We were also recently recognized by *Entrepreneur* on their coveted Entrepreneur 360 List for Innovation, Impact, and Growth. In addition, we've been involved in many amazing projects and created enormous value for others through books, speaking, and training.

I feel honored and blessed to have had the opportunity to share our strategies with people all over the world, resulting in hundreds of success stories and testimonials from people who have been helped by the information in the pages to follow. Many of these people were just getting started. Others already had huge teams and wanted even more duplication.

In other words, people just like you.

But to be successful in growing your network marketing business through social media, you must make a decision—a two-part decision, actually.

The first part is, you need to decide that network marketing is a great profession—one that you are proud of and committed to being successful in.

When I initially got started, I admit that I had a fear of network marketing. I didn't know how it worked. I had no warm market. I had no business experience. So, I was scared. Worse still, I wasn't sure I even believed in it fully. I had to mentally get past some of the stories I'd been told about the profession. I had to invest in the trainings. I needed to go to events, to see that people were making it work—that it was real. I needed to commit to the profession, my company, and the product we were offering. To be successful, you'll have to commit to it, too.

Once you fully believe in and are committed to growing your network marketing business, the second part of the big decision you'll have to make is that social media is going to be worth your time and effort.

Both parts of the decide-phase need to be in place to begin. If you don't believe in your company, your product, and your profession—and you don't believe in social media as a critical tool—you'll only achieve a fraction of the success you desire.

About the Title of This Book

When you look up the word *freakish,* one definition you'll find is: *"An oddity, something appearing in a circus sideshow."* That's not the definition of *freakish* we're suggesting, of course.

What we're describing is a second definition of *freakish* that's also right there in black and white: *"something that is markedly uncommon, unusual, or abnormal."* This is the *freakish* we're talking about.

On the pages to follow, we're going to show you something different. We're going to share exactly how to operate in other people's worlds—*in a win-win, non-spammy way*—and then draw them into yours. And to do it regularly. Consistently.

In a freakishly effective way.

So, the title isn't a sneaky way to sell more books, though we don't mind if that happens, too! It's designed to put us on the hook to deliver on that promise to provide you with a process for helping you achieve success in network marketing through social media.

There are as many ways to *do* social media as there are people. However, there are methods, concepts, and ways of doing social media that, if done, will make you way more effective.

Doing Social Media Right

The fact is, most people are doing social media the wrong way—especially in the network marketing profession. A lot of what we see out there is embarrassing, shallow, spammy marketing tactics that give the person, his or her company, and network marketing a bad name. If you can learn to do it the right way and you have the right audience to go after, then your business can skyrocket.

Sadly, there are still some leaders who think social media doesn't work, or that you don't need to learn and use it. Why? They see people posting away on social media, turning off everyone in their Facebook or Instagram network. As a result, leaders often think that if they tell their people to do social media, that this is what's going to happen to their whole team—that instead of social media making things happen, it will, instead, result in everything crumbling and falling apart.

There is also the concern that the social media approach isn't going to duplicate—that people aren't going to be able to do that online. The reason for that is, again, most people are doing it wrong.

You'll find that if you do it the right way and follow some very simple and easily duplicatable steps, you can use social media effectively. And you can create a team that duplicates like crazy.

But you must do it right.

Fears of Social Media

The fear of talking to "strangers" is a common issue within the network marketing profession. And it's no different on social media. The worry over what others are going to think exists for many people, just like it does in real-life, person-to-person, belly-to-belly sales and recruiting.

And there's a fear of putting your life *"out there"* for everyone to see. And the fear that social media is oversaturated—that it's too late to get involved or make an impact.

Yes, fear is an issue for most people. It holds us all back in one way or another. All we ask is that you set your fears aside and be open to the things we're about to share.

We think you'll be happily surprised.

"To be freakishly effective on social media, your purpose— which should be to make solid connections with people—is more important than the platform on which you are operating."

-Ray & Jessica Higdon

#FESM

(Take a picture of this page and use #FESM)

Is Social Media a Fad?

One of the things a lot of people are wondering (especially in the world of network marketing) is: *Should I invest my time and energy learning how to use social media?* What if it's just a fad and everything I put into learning it is wasted?

Let's get one thing straight: Not only is social media not a fad, it's not even all that new. Humans being *social* with one another is something we've been doing for thousands of years, since the first cave people sat around the campfire and exchanged stories. And *media,* defined as *the means of mass communication (broadcasting, publishing, etc.)* has been around since long before Guttenberg invented the press.

So, basically, social media is the process of humans interacting with other humans—which we've been doing for thousands of years—only today, it's done online. The only thing that's *new* is the scale at which people can interact with one another because of the internet.

So, no. Social media isn't a fad. And even if it changes its form (which it most certainly will), it isn't going away.

Is Traditional Marketing Dead?

One of the questions we get asked is, should people move away from traditional network marketing and shift their entire focus to social media?

To answer that, it's important to define what "traditional" means. For our purposes here, we mean everything we used to do *offline* before the arrival of online social media: one-on-one and small-group presentations, large events, sending physical information through the mail, calling people on the phone, etc.

The answer is a resounding *no*. To say traditional network marketing is dead is to say talking to people is dead. Trust us—talking to people will never be dead!

What social media brings to the party is a new *touchpoint*, a place in which we can come into contact with a lot of people. This larger relationship pool creates greater opportunities to reach out and talk to a lot more people.

In this way, social media doesn't replace traditional forms of network marketing—it merely magnifies and enhances the ability to use our traditional means more often. Put another way, social media opens the door that you invite prospects to walk through.

How Much of Your Marketing Should Be Online?

Is there a rule of thumb to follow as to what percentage of your marketing efforts should conducted on social media versus other methods? 20%? 50%? 80%?

There is no hard-and-fast number that applies to everyone. Some people have achieved significant levels of success spending 100% of their time online. Others have achieved equal levels of success and wouldn't know how to set up a Facebook page to save their lives.

Trying to determine the right social media/traditional marketing split is like asking what percentage of your exercise should be on the treadmill versus what percentage of your exercise should be done lifting weights. It depends on the person and their goals.

The key questions are: What is the best way to connect with a large quantity of people, big enough to grow your business at the pace you desire? And what marketing and recruiting activities do you enjoy enough so it's easy to stick with them until you see results? Answer these questions and it will be more clear why both marketing approaches matter.

What Platforms Should You Be On?

The mix of platforms you are on is up to you, depending on your desires and personal strengths.

If there's a platform you feel comfortable with—one you like and believe you can do the most with—then go for it. Anywhere that there's people, you can build a business. That said, learn the technical aspects of that platform because there are different ways to communicate with people on each.

Also, spend the most time on the platform that has the type of people you are most trying to attract and then be aware that this platform could change. For example, right now more millennials (people in the 18 to 32 age range) are on Instagram and Snapchat than on Facebook. However, we built the majority of our business using Facebook.

Regardless of which platform you choose, just be sure you become someone who shares a lot of value (which we will cover in detail in just a bit).

The fundamentals we're sharing in this book will work just about anywhere. That's why they're called *fundamentals*. Once you understand how to apply the psychology behind the process of selling and recruiting people online, you can do it on whatever platform you want. So, work with the one that you feel most comfortable with.

Changing Trends in Popular Platforms

The big trend, at the time of this writing, is the wild increase in the use of live video as a means of getting content out. This trend is almost certain to grow. Until it doesn't.

Because trends are always changing. And, undoubtedly, next year, there will be some new social media fad. There will be "Snappers" or "Boggle" or something else. There will be some kind of breakthrough technology where you can do live videos even better—something we can't even imagine yet—and there will be people who will be on it.

To be freakishly effective on social media, your purpose—which should be to make solid connections with people—is more important than the platform on which you are operating.

Don't Try to Be Everywhere

On the other hand, just because we say it's okay to be *anywhere*, you shouldn't try to be *everywhere*. Trying to be on every single platform will dissipate your influence (hurting your results) and leave you feeling exhausted (which might make you feel like quitting altogether).

This is not to say you can't be everywhere eventually. Once you get a foothold on a couple platforms and begin to get results, you can outsource certain activities, which will allow you to expand. But not right away. Not when you're first getting started. In the beginning, the goal is to be lean and focused.

"Marketing" Versus "Prospecting"

In terms of building your network marketing business, social media serves two major purposes: marketing and prospecting.

These are not just two different words for the same activity. Marketing and prospecting are very different, and you need to learn to do both on social media.

MARKETING is when you do something that you hope an unnamed individual reacts or responds to. It could be a status update, image, video, flyer, advertisement, billboard, etc. Marketing is passive where you hope someone takes action from it that notifies you in some way.

PROSPECTING is when you reach out to an individual, online or offline, cold market (people you don't know) or warm market (friends and family members). It is YOU at least attempting to start a conversation with an individual.

Many people only think of social media as a place to market themselves, where you communicate something that you hope people will react or respond to.

This is half of the social media equation.

The other part, which is often overlooked, is the act of prospecting for people on various social media platforms. We know many people who have built large organizations and have made a lot of money on social media but who have also never posted content. How? They've become exceptionally good at prospecting. They use social media to reach out to people, to connect and find out if the person is open to hearing about an opportunity.

Don't get us wrong. We are big fans of social media marketing, meaning posting content in the hopes that someone sees it and private messages you. Maybe it's a blog post, maybe it's a video. Maybe it's a Facebook Live broadcast or an ad. We're not trying to minimize the importance of these activities—they are all effective for the purposes of attracting people to you, and these activities are also a big part of how we've grown our company.

But when we work with people at our live events and in our Rank Makers group, we also teach people to use social media for prospecting.

Prospecting is *proactive*, when you reach out directly to an individual on one of the social media platforms—like Facebook or LinkedIn—and when you initiate the conversation by sending private messages to connect with people to see if they're open to the next step, which is seeing a presentation.

Both marketing and prospecting are effective. And you should do both.

It's About Connecting

Without a doubt, being "social" on social media is important to success. But let's not forget that, at the end of the day, the purpose of being on social media is to sell product, build a team, and—yes—make money.

We need to connect with people who will become customers and/or join our teams.

Think building valuable connections through social media is easy? Even people who are good at communicating with others face to face, in the "real" world often forget that on the other side of an online interaction or social media exchange is a real person, another human being with the same goals, dreams and needs that we have. People we are trying to attract to us. People we are trying to get to take the next step with us.

Look at the sentence below. Without looking ahead (in other words, without cheating), see if your mind automatically fills in the blanks:

All things being equal, people prefer to do business with people they _____, _____, and _____.

Easy, right? 90% of the people who saw the statement will have filled in the blanks as follows:

All things being equal, people prefer to do business with people they _know_, _like_, and _trust_.

That's what you should be thinking about when sharing on social media. Ask yourself:

- *Is what I am about to communicate going to increase the feeling in others that they know me?*

- *Will it increase the likelihood that they will like me?*

- *And does it have a significant chance of increasing their level of trust?*

In a perfect world, every piece of social media communication you create has a positive impact on all three of these social media success factors. At a minimum, your communications positively impact two of the three.

The Attention/Connection Challenge

When it comes to social media, the challenge is getting positive attention and connecting in a positive way. In terms of a formula, think of it as:

Positive Attention + *Positive* Connection

= *Positive* Results

Conversely:

Negative Attention + *Negative* Connection

= *Negative* Results

(Note: In this case, a negative and a negative is not a positive. This isn't math. It's social media.)

You Don't Have to Be a "Brand"

The concept of *branding* gets thrown around a lot these days, so much so that you can't help but think that this is the goal of being on social media. It's not. You don't have to *have* a brand or *be* a brand to achieve success. All you need to do is create communications and connections that help you hit your numbers.

When we first started, branding on social media wasn't being talked about much, so we just worked on hitting the number of communications we wanted to send every single day. Not only did we have zero experience in building a brand, we didn't

"The number-one marketing error is focusing on what YOU have instead of focusing on what others struggle with or want. Focus on what others are looking for, then connect with them to what you have."

-Ray & Jessica Higdon

#FESM

(Take a picture of this page and use #FESM)

even know what our brand was or should be. We just kept pushing out quality content that we knew would help people. (We'll talk more about quality content later!)

In our case—with no intention of building a brand—our brand was built anyway. Our consistent flow of quality content simply morphed into a brand, all on its own.

The only brand elements you need to focus on is providing value on a consistent basis. In our case, this turned into a training platform, then a company. But it didn't happen overnight. Consistency was the key—a level of consistency that built trust.

Your Company Is <u>Not</u> Your Brand

It's important to realize that your network marketing company is not your brand. Your company may be truly great, but you will diminish your results if you are branding your network marketing company.

When people join a business, even as a customer, they are joining *you*—what *you* stand for and what *you* represent. People make a huge mistake when they brand themselves too much to their company and/or their product. Here's what we mean:

Pretend for a moment that you're not selling anything that has to do with your company. Focus on being passionate about your message, whether that's family...or health...or whatever.

Maybe you're a woman who is passionate about makeup and making women feel confident and beautiful. Maybe you're a man who is passionate about diet and nutrition. Whatever the message for you may be, picture yourself sharing that passion by communicating information to others who may be interested in the same thing, without there being any product, service, or company attached.

Just imagine posting videos—interesting information you've come across, cool recipes, great workouts, etc.—each of which is intended to be of interest to the types of people you are trying to attract. By creating videos or status updates that help them with their problems, you will attract them to you and put them in a place to want to know more about you and what you are doing.

The Person / Product Connection

Now, this is not to say there should be <u>no</u> connection between the things you post and your product, service, and/or company. Of course, there should be.

But we've discovered it is infinitely better to focus on things *you* are personally interested in and then to help educate or solve the problem(s) of the type of person you want to attract without talking about your products or company directly.

That said, here's a little word of caution: It is harder to become an authority in a broader market (e.g., "inspiration") than in something that's more specific. So, if you're looking to be an expert or authority in a given area, the closer you can niche down, the better.

When I *(this is Jessica again)* first started doing video, I got some views here and there, some comments, some leads—even some sign-ups. But I noticed that when I focused on the people

I wanted to attract and how I could help them solve their problems my views went through the roof!

The best part was, I loved talking about it! So, in a way, you might say my audience told me what they wanted to see more of. And because what I loved talking about was congruent with making connections and building my business, my leads went through the roof, too.

The takeaway? Say, for example, you are wanting to attract someone who wants to lose weight. Focus your social media efforts around attracting and helping them.

Also, remember, the key thing is to start. Don't get hung up on your brand. Just get out there and start talking about things you're passionate about—sharing what you care about and what you know.

Setting Up Your Facebook Profile

As with everything else on social media, there are countless ways to set up your profile. But is there a right way? Yes—or, let's just say there are things you can do that will attract people to you and move your business forward.

Many people in network marketing have a job in addition to the business they are building—that's how most of us start. Given this, your Facebook profile should have the following two objectives:

- To set up a profile that doesn't put your job in jeopardy
- To set up a profile that helps you build your business and create the desire in others to want to work with you in your network marketing business.

Both objectives need to be served at the same time...in the same profile.

Controlling Your Public Image

Think of your profile as your first impression. It's like somebody meeting you for the first time at a party. If you walk into a party with three drinks in your hand and you're slurring your words...or your hair is messed up and your clothes are wrinkled...people are going to make assumptions. *About you.*

The assumptions people make may be correct, or *not* correct. Worse still, the assumptions people make are out of your control. But the *basis* for those assumptions are completely under your control—*which is entirely on you.*

The Visual Aspects of Your Profile

First, take the time to make sure your profile is visually appealing. People are busy today and easily distracted. They're online looking at 10 things at once. You need to have images that grab attention and say the right things about you.

Your Facebook banner should be an image that represents who you are. This may be a picture of you, or you with family and friends. Or it might be a combination of sports and/or lifestyle images. What sport do you love? How does that sport play into your lifestyle? If you're a water skier, post pictures of you water skiing.

Do you love chess? Create a banner with a picture of a chess board. Better yet, create a banner with a picture of *you* playing chess.

As for your profile picture, make it of you.

We love our daughter more than anything in the world, but we're not going to put our daughter's picture where our picture should be because when we're reaching out to people and posting things, people will associate everything we do with our daughter. We also love our dogs, but we're not going to put a profile picture of our dog. Why not? Everybody loves dogs, right? No, not everybody.

We want people to associate and connect with *us*. They're going to be dealing with us, not our daughter and certainly not our dog.

That does not mean you can't use family photos! But when it comes to *your* profile picture, just don't use a picture that does not include you. Don't use that special profile picture for a logo, cartoon, or anything but your face. (It is *Facebook* after all!)

Another thing to consider: We love a nice glass of wine or a bottle of beer every now and then. But we're not going to post pictures of ourselves drinking everywhere on our Facebook pages. In fact, when people go to take pictures with us, or we're taking pictures of ourselves, we try and keep alcohol out of the picture.

Again, it's not that there's anything wrong having a few drinks. But you never know who's going to be turned off by that.

Now, are there exceptions to this? Yes. For example, let's say you are with a direct selling company and the product is wine—well, there is your exception!

The point is, show images that help you attract the people you want to attract, without unnecessarily repelling others.

Your Profile Information

Your profile information on any platform comes down to two things:

1. Who are you?

2. Why should someone stick around?

The first question is straightforward and requires only that you tell visitors things about yourself that you want shared: What do you do? What do you believe in? Things of this nature.

It's question #2 that requires more careful consideration.

Answering why someone should stick around requires you to think about the specific ways in which you help people. That's why someone should stick around. The big question is, would *you* follow you?

If you go to a profile and learn what city someone lives in or that they have three kids, that's just background. It's good to know, but so what? Everyone's got a story, and that is theirs.

But if that person mentions he or she happens to be an award-winning real estate agent and has helped three people sell their homes in the last month, well, this might be somebody you want to work with in the future. You make a mental note. Why? Because they're not just someone with a miscellaneous set of background details—*they're someone who might be able to help you.*

The truth, whether we want to admit it or not, is that we're always on the lookout for people who may be able to help us in some way. And it's the same concept when it comes to network marketing, which is why your Intro on Facebook should be about how what you do helps people.

Your Headline

Your headline, which can be applied to your Facebook banner or on LinkedIn, is very important because that's the next thing people see when they see your name. By the way, if you do have a link to a website, it should be generic, not your company website.

The best way to create a headline is to claim your niche. Ideally, it's your niche plus your specific benefit or focus area.

- Example Headline: *Gluten-free nutrition expert.*

- Better Example: *Gluten-free nutrition expert helping busy people eat healthy and lose weight with an easy regimen that actually tastes good.*

You can see that if people are interested in this area, they would be instantly drawn to you. Whatever you do, avoid being too generic or using phrases you see everywhere like, "health and wellness expert" or "lifestyle coach." They are overused. The more targeted and specific, the better. You can also add something called a "proof point" to make what you do even more compelling and real.

Example: A travel and vacation expert who helps people take luxury vacations on a shoestring budget and saved the average couple $3,800 last year.

Note: We were over a million a year before we had a tagline or logo. The biggest mistake we see made in this area is people taking forever to try to get their tagline/logo/brand perfect. Figure it out down the road but, in the meantime, be prospecting and creating attractive content.

Your Company

When people see your company name, they will Google it and then draw their own conclusions. And what do we find when we Google anything? Probably something negative!

So, you may be wondering, where do I get to share information about my company in my profile?

A lot of times people look at a big leader's profile and see the company everywhere. They see it on the banner and in the intro. They see things about the company and products on all the leader's posts.

And guess what? The big leader is getting tons of likes and shares. So, it's easy to assume that is how you should position your profile. The only problem is, almost all of those likes and shares are not prospects—they are from other people in the company. The leader has built a massive reputation within the company, often being on stages training and getting a ton of recognition. This person has built that audience based on what he or she has already done, the rank achieved, and the momentum gained from that leadership status and reputation.

So, it's easy to think, if I do that too, that will happen to me. Sorry, not going to happen. It will likely just turn people off from you.

You should <u>not</u> have the name of your company or product all over your social media account, because it hurts you in a couple of ways. If there's plenty of information on what you do, and what product and company you're a part of on your social media account, then your customers and prospects can and will go do their own independent research. They don't need to reach out to you and have a conversation, which is what more network marketers should be striving for.

Instead of automatic sign-ups, you should be aiming for more conversations, where people are reaching out to you or you are reaching out to others to start a conversation and see if someone is open to your business. That will usually not happen if you have your company name or product name all over your social media account.

That said, if there is a top leader doing social media using automatic sign-ups, that's awesome, and he or she should keep doing that if it's working. For you, go a different route because you haven't built up those connections and followers yet.

This book doesn't dive into the intricacies of team building and duplication, but look for a future book on this, and tune into our trainings inside of Rank Makers by checking out WhatIsRankMakers.com.

"Social media is the greatest—and unfortunately, the worst— thing to happen to network marketing. It took the pro to another level of being able to connect, converse, and prospect, and it took the amateur to new levels of annoying and spamming the masses."

-Ray & Jessica Higdon

#FESM

(Take a picture of this page and use #FESM)

Identify Your Target Audience

Most people think of social media as an ocean filled with millions of prospects swimming around, just waiting to be caught up in your net.

Casting a wide net may feel like it's the most effective way to operate. But it's not. Remember, everyone is not right for you... *and you are not right for everyone.* So, don't go out on social media with the mindset that you are trying to reach everybody.

- You have *your* specific and unique situation: man, woman, married, single, kids, no kids, younger, older, and on and on...

- You have *your* specific and unique personality.

- You have *your* specific and unique message.

Social media is a place to use your uniqueness to your advantage. This is central to allowing your message to break through the clutter, attracting people with whom your message and uniqueness resonates.

It's important to remember you're not trying to get anyone and everyone into your business. Identifying your target market helps you recognize who great prospects are when they come to you, which helps you determine with whom you really want to spend time.

Commit to Delivering Value

Now, it's time to commit to creating a certain number of value-oriented posts per day or per week, either on your profile, your fan page, or in groups.

What do we mean by "value-oriented" posts? We mean delivering content that is of perceived value to your target audience, with no expectation of immediate return.

- *That means no links!*
- *That means no mention of your company!*
- *That means no mention of your product!*
- No sales hype *("ground floor opportunity", "no competition", "it's super-easy", etc.)*

Only valuable posts, as determined in the mind of the audience you are trying to influence. And you must determine the number of posts you intend to deliver—per day and/or per week—to ensure that you are not only delivering value but are doing so consistently.

Do you need to go public with your commitment? Do you need to tell your audience they can expect a post on certain days and at certain times? No. But you do need to have an *internal* number of posts that you are committed to delivering.

Posting for Profits

When you post, it is possible to get people interested in what you have and begin buying from you. It will take some time to build up an audience, but there is a way to do it strategically through your posts.

But first, we want to tackle a myth—or, more accurately, a misunderstanding. And that misunderstanding is that a lead is only someone who comes through a funnel.

A lead is anybody that raises their hand by showing an interest in what you've shared on social media. This could be someone who likes your post, shares your post, messages you, calls you, or simply comments. It doesn't matter. *Anyone who shows interest in what you have is a lead.*

The goal of any post is to get more people to show interest and raise their hand, whether it's something on the product side or on the business side. Remember, marketing is passive and is where you are posting or creating something you hope an unnamed individual reacts or responds to while prospecting is you reaching out to an individual to see if they are open to what you have to offer. Don't just rely on who responds to your marketing. Be sure to get your prospecting numbers in as well!

Five Types of Posts

There are five major types of posts, which can be done as videos or as text posts:

1. Value Posts

Value posts are extremely important because they get your ideal prospects—people in your target market—following you. To do that, your content must have value and be relevant.

Now, you might be wondering: *What do you mean by value?*

Value posts provide solutions to common problems—problems that are shared by a large group of people. As a result, your posts answer the "W.I.I.F.M." question: the question that goes through the mind of anyone who is exploring virtually anything online. And that question is:

What's In It For Me?

You must assume that people are asking themselves: *Why should I spend my time reading your posts or watching your videos?*

The answer should always be: *Because the things you are sharing are of interest to them.*

Posting content of value to others not only gets people to pay attention to what you are sharing and engage with you, they also get people to follow you and look forward to your posts! They also motivate them to visit your page often so when you do finally ask them to take some form of action, or make a little "pitch" at some point, they are willing listen to what you have to say because you've been giving them so much value for so long.

For a value video post, we suggest using a very simple formula:

- *Intro*

- *Question*

- *Content*

- *Call to Action*

For example:

> *"Hi, my name is Jessica Higdon, and do you ever wonder, what in the world I should be posting throughout the day? Today I'm going to be sharing with you five types of posts that you can use to post throughout the day, and I'm going to give you the exact formulas for those."*

You would then do your teaching (share your tip) and close out the video with a call to action statement, something like:

> *"If you loved this training, feel free to reach out to me. You can message me directly via my inbox. I check each and every message personally."*

Telling people that you check each and every email personally is extremely effective. It's even more impactful once someone has come to know, like and trust you because of your history of providing value on a consistent basis. You must be willing, of course, to fulfill that promise and take the time to look at and respond to every message.

2. Recognition Post

Recognition is an incredible tool, if done properly, to get people interested in your product or service.

In this type of post, what you want to do is tell a story of some kind. The reason you want to tell a story is that stories draw people in. And they allow you to provide *social proof* of how your product, service, and/or company is making a positive impact on others and changing lives in subtle ways.

Here's an example of a recognition post:

> *"Congratulations to Suzi who just earned a brand-new BMW! Suzi was a kindergarten teacher who wanted to spend more time at home with her family, so she sought out a home-based business. She now works full time from home and is driving her dream car. So proud of this amazing woman. If you're curious how*

Suzi did it, feel free to private message me."

Providing social proof is the number one way on social media to recruit someone. Plus, in the above example, notice the call to action at the end. The key here is to make your call to action subtle and not overly direct or aggressive, like: *"Join my team!"*

It isn't: *"If you're curious how Suzi did it, feel free to check out my product website here."*

It's: *"Feel free to <u>reach out to me</u>."*

Another thing about providing social proof is the way in which it naturally arouses curiosity in others—curiosity that turns into leads for your business. You're providing recognition, which is a form of social proof, but the mind of the reader is wondering, *"How? How did they do that? I'm curious."*

What you do <u>not</u> want to do with recognition is say, *"Hey, here's Bob. Bob joined my team three days ago and now he's made $1 million, and if you want to join my team, join here."*

This is a terrible recognition post. Why? Because even if it's true, it smells like spam. Anything that smells like spam is not good. Even if it's true, posts like this will not be believed.

Also, recognition posts must be done sparingly. Don't overdo them. They are best when sprinkled here and there, maybe a couple times throughout the week. If you do them every day, people will get tired of seeing them, and they will stop paying attention.

3. Story Post

The third type of post is a story post. The story in this post may be about you, or about someone you know, and usually ends with a call to action. That action could be to message you for more information, or to check out a website to learn more. If it's your own story, be willing to be vulnerable and share your struggle.

The first sentence should be a powerful attention grabber—a dramatic statement, perhaps. For example: *"Live events changed my life."*

You can also accomplish the same goal through an intriguing question: *"Can a live event change your life?"*

Then all you do is tell a story about how a live event impacted you. For example: *"I struggled for years to build my business, and then I attended an event and _____ happened."*

The story becomes an obvious tie-in to the live event you're promoting and sets up the perfect call to action.

And the more dramatic and life-changing, the better. For example, you could tell a story about how you found your first leader:

> *"I was literally in the fetal position, balling my eyes out on the bathroom floor because I was so frustrated with how many people I was reaching out to and nobody was joining my business. But I didn't give up. A couple weeks after that, I found my first leader and got things rolling. So, here's what helped me find my first leader."*

Notice that the story you tell doesn't have to be about you—it can be about what happened to someone else. In that way, you can share a virtually endless number of stories!

4. Engagement Post

Engagement posts are designed to get interaction from the people to whom you are connected. There are an infinite number of ways to create engagement. For example, you can post a funny photo and ask people to "caption this photo." Anything that makes people "fill in the blank" is a great way to get them to interact and engage. For example:

- *My favorite food is _____.*
- *The best action movie is _____.*
- *The one person in all of history I would like to have dinner with is _____.*

An engagement post is a fun and easy way to create interaction. It's also a good way to help people feel they know you, and for you to get to know them, too!

5. Call to Action Post

Call to action posts are done less frequently because they are posts where you are giving a pitch. It could be that you're pitching free content, a free article, or whatever. With this kind of post, it's okay to get straight to the point. It's obvious that you're pitching something, so just get right to it and let people know exactly what you're offering and what they need to do to get it.

You can also mix a little engagement in with a call to action. For example: *"If you want to learn how to _____, send me a message and I'll shoot you a free report."* Or, *"If I wanted to lose five pounds by next week, I would do this very simple tip. Click the link here to learn what it is."*

Be authentic and vulnerable at times. Remember: The more value you put out, the better results you'll get from your marketing. Be a problem solver, not a pusher. That means find ways to provide value, never pushing people but pulling them toward you.

You only want to do call to action posts about 10% of the time, and they're most effective when you've been using the four other types of posts for a while first.

Consistency and Congruency

When it comes to having success with the posts you create, it's important to maintain consistency and congruency.

In terms of consistency, a good goal for building a network marketing business via social media would be to consistently do a minimum of one to two posts per day.

Fact is, most people don't even post once a day, so if you can get in the habit of posting something of value one to two times a day, you'll be doing twice what others are doing. Consistency is what wins the game when it comes to marketing on social media. And it is this consistency that will eventually yield a consistent flow of leads.

In addition to consistency, pay attention to *congruency*. In other words, don't post recipes one day, then talk about franchising the next. For example, just imagine how sharing methods for taking care of your skin, then suddenly changing direction to tips of improving skiing skills would leave people seriously confused.

As you plan your posts, make sure they're in harmony with one another, each revolving around a central theme or topic area—whatever it is you want to be known for. If you stay congruent in everything you do, people will come to see you as an authority in your subject area, rather than someone who simply shares a bunch of scattered content and messages.

What Should You Talk About?

People get frustrated trying to decide which direction to take. They struggle to figure out what area of expertise deserves their focus. Understandably, everyone wants to know what works "best." So here is the answer in case you are struggling with the same question.

Instead of trying to decide what will work best, ask yourself: *What do I want to talk about?* Asking, '*what works*' is the wrong question because almost anything will work if you do it well and do it consistently.

What you should talk about are the things that get you fired up. If you like talking about exercises to get six-pack abs, then talk about that. If you get fired up talking about entrepreneurship, communication, cooking, sales, marketing, beauty tips, whatever—then rock that out.

Check Yourself Before You Wreck Yourself

One of the traps that is easy to fall into—especially if you're trying to create a lot of content fast—is to allow some reckless, inappropriate posts to slip through. By this, we mean things that might hurt your image, your reputation, and your chances for success.

Imagine watching someone online for a long period of time and thinking: *This person is pretty interesting, and they're providing valuable information.* And then, suddenly, that individual posts something that destroys everything they've worked hard to build—something like:

- *Posting a video of themselves getting embarrassingly drunk at a party*

- *Launching into an out-of-the-blue and an overly-nasty religious or political rant*

- *Calling out a competitor or hating on them (especially with expletive-laced language)*

There are only two reasons someone would post any of the above-mentioned things: 1) to attract attention and 2) because this person is just not thinking. Yes, you want attention—but not the wrong kind of attention. You need to be thinking like someone who might be watching you from afar—because they are.

People will often watch you for a long time before they finally decide to reach out. There are some people watching you who could become some of your biggest producers. When we were building our network marketing team years ago, we had someone join who ended up doing extremely well and then one day casually mentioned: *"I watched you for six months before I finally reached out to you."*

Previewing Every Post

Before you post anything, stop and ask yourself: *If **you** were looking to work with somebody and **they** posted what you're about to post, would **you** want to work with you? Would **you** be attracted to you?*

And just so we're clear, the things you post don't have to be overtly over-the-top obnoxious to push people away. It could be something as simple as saying, *"Wow, my spouse is really nagging me lately."* The good news is there will be a segment of people on social media who will be understanding, some of whom will reach out and comment on how their spouses nag them, too.

The bad news is there will be a much bigger portion of the social media viewing public that will write you off as a jerk for making a negative public comment about your spouse and start ignoring everything you say from that point forward.

Here's another example: You innocently say, *"Man, it really sucks having to work today."* Yes, there is a large section of the public who would agree with you. But professionals are good, solid, hardworking people who don't complain about having a job because they recognize there are unemployed people out there who would kill to have a job—*any job.* Besides, who wants to join someone's team when all they do is complain?

The Magic of Being Real

Here's an interesting question. *Which is more important: appearing polished and professional, or real and accessible?*

The answer to this is easy: When it comes to connecting with people on social media, your primary goal should be to appear accessible.

You're not out there selling TVs or automobiles or appliances. You're really selling the idea that people can do what you do. And the key to that is to present yourself as real and relatable, authentic and vulnerable. *Yes, vulnerable.*

Why? Because, at our core, we're *all* a bit vulnerable. We're human beings. So, if you're trying to build a network marketing business made up of a collection of humans, present yourself as human. Not superhuman. Not Superman or Superwoman. Just a normal person.

The underlying goal of everything you communicate is to have people say, *"Hey, if this person can do it, I can do it too."* It isn't to have people saying, *"Wow! I wish I was good enough to do what they're doing."*

If you think the goal is to impress others with how special you are, then you've missed the point entirely. You want everyone you touch to come away thinking, "I can do that!" Because this business isn't just about the ability to duplicate yourself—it's about the *belief* in the ability to duplicate yourself.

Sharing Your Pain and Circumstances

You might be wondering then, should I post about the challenges I have in my life? There's always a place for challenges. Perhaps. But if you do, be careful. You don't want to come from a place of self-pity, whether justified or not, for example, going on social media and saying, *"Everything sucks, my life is a disaster. Everything always seems to happen to me! Why me? Why me?"*

The truth is, few people simply respond well to that type of post—at least not the type of people you want on your team. And they won't be inspired to join your team, either. But if you say, *"Hey, I'm going through this right now, and I want everyone to know if there's anybody out there who's going through the same thing, you can do this, it's alright, it's going to be okay, let's power through this together."* You will find that (at least most) people will rally behind you. They'll likely be able to relate to your problems because they have problems, too.

So, don't be afraid to share how you're feeling, just be careful how you share it. Keep everything positive, even when things aren't going well, versus overtly complaining and searching for sympathy.

"Posting how much money can be easily made by your network marketing company is sort of like showing too much cleavage on social media. It WILL get you attention but often not the type you are hoping for!"

-Ray & Jessica Higdon

#FESM

(Take a picture of this page and use #FESM)

The Importance of Video

When it comes to creating content, there is no better way than doing video. Video is a little more involved than a text or image post, but it is the very best form of marketing when it comes to giving value and attracting people to you.

Because when it comes to having people feel they know, like, and trust you, nothing is as effective as video, short of driving to their house and sitting in their living room.

Now, you may be thinking, *"But I don't want to do video. Do I have to?"* No, you don't have to use it, but it's kind of like using a riding lawnmower vs. using an old, rusted-out, hard-to-push, manual lawnmower. You can cut your yard without a riding power mower, but why would you?

If you want more people to connect with you and see your message in its best form, then video is the most powerful way to do that.

At this moment, the easiest way to do video is Facebook Live. Before Facebook Live, you would shoot a video, upload it, and hope that someone would see it. Now, you press one button and instantly people all over the world can watch. It is hands-down the fastest and easiest way to get in front of a live audience that has ever existed.

The Freakishly Effective
Four-Step Video Formula

Whether it's for Facebook Live or in other social media platforms, there is a tried and true formula for running any video, and it's comprised of four simple steps:

1) **Introduction**

2) **Question**

3) **Content**

4) **Call to Action ("CTA")**

We covered all this briefly in the "Value Post" section, but it's so key for video, we want to break it down even further. Let's look at each in more detail.

1. Introduction

The number-one, most effective intro is to simply say, *"Hi, my name is* _____*."* This should not be followed by what rank you're at in your company, nor should there be any mention of how much you're worth or how much money you're making per month. Your intro is not your resume—it's just who you are.

And even if you've been on social media for years, it's important to say your name before you get started. Yes, people may know you already, but the repetition of having them hear your name is not only good marketing, it also guarantees someone who may be seeing and hearing you for the first time knows who you are, as well.

2. Question

Next, give the person watching a reason to keep watching. This is best done by asking a *benefit-driven question* that is aimed to keep and retain the type of person you're trying to reach.

For example, if you're trying to attract people who want to lose weight, it would sound like this:

"Hi, my name is Ray Higdon. Hey, are you trying to stop nighttime sugar cravings? Well, stick around and I'm going to share some tips with you on how to do just that."

3. Content

This is the portion of the video where you share content that fulfills the promise you just made.

The tips you provide may be something you've done yourself, something you've read in a book, or they could be things you pulled off Google.

It isn't critical for you to know everything about a subject to share what you've learned—even if you just learned it five minutes ago. Just share what you've learned.

In this way, it's possible for virtually anyone to come across as a guru on just about anything without having to *be* a guru, by simply spending a little bit of time doing research.

And another thing: No one cares if what you're sharing is your original content, they just want the content. All you have to do is say, *"Hey, I was just reading this month's Prevention Magazine and it says these three tips will help you with nighttime sugar cravings."* In all the years that we have shared third-party content, we have never had a single person say, *"Oh my god, I can't believe you can't come up with your own stuff."*

To be clear: We are not saying you should ever present

someone else's content as your own. You should always identify the sources of the material you're sharing. At a minimum, you should say something like, *"I'm reading this new book and learned about XYZ topic,"* even if you don't name the title of the book or the book's author. That said, amazing things CAN happen. I don't think my book, "Go for No! for Network Marketing" would exist if I hadn't given the authors credit!

4. Call to Action

Finally, what exactly do you want people to do? Where should they go to learn more? What action(s) do you want them to take?

In some cases, you want to direct people to a way to stay engaged with and connected to you. For example: *"Hope this tip helped you, and please be sure to comment and share this post with anyone else you think could benefit."*

Or...

"I hope you got a little something out of my video. I would love to stay connected with you...please click on the link and sign up to get notified about my videos and other cool stuff I am sharing."

Every now and then, you can add in an actual pitch about your business. For example, you could say, *"Hey everyone! Here's your inspirational tip of the day!"*

After you share your tip, you can follow it up with something like: *"Oh, by the way, many of you are on here, and I love it that you appreciate my inspirational posts, and my motivation. I hope it lifts you up! By the way, you may or may not know this, but I have a home business where I'm constantly looking for sharp individuals that are hungry to make money from home, even on a very part-time basis. If that sounds like you, feel free to reach out to me. I'd be more than happy to chat with you. And just know, it may not be a good fit for you. Maybe you're not even open to it at all. And if not, totally cool. Keep enjoying the inspiration. Talk to you guys later."*

Finding Topics for Facebook Live

If part of your social media strategy is to do a daily Facebook Live, how do you possibly pick a different topic every day? The answer is, you must get totally and completely immersed in your profession and your subject.

That's where Google comes in. Trust us, there is an endless quantity of information on any topic you can imagine on Google. Then all you need to do is:

I.L.T.

ILT stands for:

- *__Invest__ your time (and perhaps a bit of money, depending on what you need to learn how to do)*

- *__Learn__ what it is you need to know, and then*

- *__Teach__ it!*

The good news is, this process makes it fast and easy. And it eliminates the excuse many people use, which is, *"But I don't know anything to teach."*

So, figure out what it is you want to teach, something that can be connected to your product, service, and opportunity. Then simply Google it and find tips! In some cases, you might want to invest in attending a seminar or taking a course or working with a coach or finding a mentor. Next, learn and master it, whatever it might be. And then teach it to others who are looking for the information and/or skills you've just acquired.

Since we launched our Rank Makers group, we've gone live with a new training every single day, along with a short, easy-to-accomplish action step. Total time investment: approximately 15 minutes per day, with huge impact.

So, if you're serious about using social media to your advantage, get immersed in your topic. And if all else fails, Google it.

Making People Curious

One of the main ways to draw people in, is to create a sense of curiosity around what you're about to say. You want them to want to know more.

Things that stimulate curiosity include stuff that is new, different, odd, amazing, weird, useful, exciting, surprising, and strange. Also:

- Secrets that others know, and they don't
- Social "chatter" (what others are talking about)
- What others have, and how they got it
- Current trends, puzzles, and mysteries

- Stories about how someone solved a problem

The goal is do short videos that show part of something, without trying to show them everything. This is how you draw people toward you, by giving them a bite-sized appetizer-portion of information—a taste of what you know—without feeling the need to give them the whole meal. Share just enough to satisfy them temporarily, but leave them wanting more from you.

Repurposing Your Content

Once you're active in social media, it won't take long to discover that some of the content you create works better than other content.

As you go, you'll develop a "backlist" of your best, most helpful and popular content. You took the time to create the content. It's yours, you own it! It's ridiculous to tuck it away in a file on your computer—never to see the light of day again. For example, when we talk about the psychology behind closing, well, things about mindset rarely change—it's what we call "evergreen" content that never gets old. It still gets results, so why wouldn't we continue to use it?

What Personality Should You Project?

One of the things you've probably noticed on social media these days is lots of people trying to get attention, taking selfies in all sorts of places and ways, jumping off waterfalls, eating live insects, and on and on.

Why?

The first reason is obvious: to get attention. The other reason is they are trying to create some sort of social media personality for themselves.

So, what is the best social media personality for you? The personality you already have. Because the personality you already have is certainly good enough all by itself.

If you think you're going to develop a following by posting videos of you delivering money-making tips standing next to a rented Lambo, you're fooling yourself. Also, projecting a false lifestyle in an attempt to lead people into believing they can have what you have—especially if you're suggesting they can get results quickly and easily—well, you could find yourself in a legal problem. So, don't do it.

That said, if you've achieved enormous success and feel the desire to show people the things you've accumulated, then have at it. That's your decision (and who are we to say you shouldn't).

The key, however, is to always remember the goal: to appear honest and accessible. So, be careful.

The other exception to the rule is, let's say you are an adventure seeker wanting to attract other adventurous people to you. Showing yourself jumping off cliffs and skydiving could be exactly the right personality to project. If something is already part of your lifestyle and an honest projection of who you really are, then have at it. If it's not, however, then it won't feel authentic.

Get rid of the idea that you must create some kind of "internet persona" that you think people will be attracted to. Real people in real settings, talking to their cell phone in an honest way about something important to them—that's what sells best.

And it's probably what's best for you, too.

Teaching Trumps Personality

We find that when it comes to marketing on social media, teaching is more duplicatable than personality.

Yes, there are some very effective, big personalities on social media, but these people are what author Malcolm Gladwell refers to as *outliers*. The folks are people who are on the fringe, outside of the norm. They use tactics that rely on charisma and showy, over-the-top antics.

There are a lot of "outliers" in network marketing who have crushed it on social media by using personality and charisma. They tell people, *"Just go out there and be a hoot—be fun, be energetic, do things that get attention."*

There are problems with this approach.

First and foremost, we find most people aren't comfortable trying to duplicate someone else's way of doing something, especially if it forces them outside their comfort zone, so they just won't do it.

Trying to become a social media "personality" seems like a good idea at first, but even if you have the personality to pull it off, it's very difficult to duplicate.

From our experience, anyone with any kind of personality—big and bold, or quiet and unassuming—can succeed on social media *if* they are delivering great content and providing information and/or teaching something others are interested in.

And letting people be themselves is totally duplicatable.

People don't solely watch content to be entertained. There are lots of forms of entertainment out there. TV. Movies. Cat videos. People are also willing to watch your content to learn something. So, teach! If you've got a strong, contagious personality, that's great—it might help, and most certainly it won't hurt. But in the end, providing information of value trumps being entertained. You don't have to be super charismatic on video—if you are addressing solutions to problems people have, they will find value in you.

The Ideal "Mix" of Information and Entertainment

One of the reasons reality TV is so popular is because people want to see inside the lives of other people. In the same way, they'll want to live vicariously through you, and be on your journey, too.

Remember, to build a successful network marketing organization, you don't have to impress anyone. You do have to connect with people and get them to believe they can do what you are doing. Keep showing up and giving value and others will want to learn more—that is when you point them to your company video or tool. If your company or your upline does not offer (or have) an effective video presentation or tool, we teach strategies in our Team Building course at HigdonGroup.com/teambuilder (along with how to create a fast-start training and more).

"To build a successful network marketing organization, you don't have to impress anyone. You do have to connect and get them to believe they can do what you are doing."

-Ray & Jessica Higdon

#FESM

(Take a picture of this page and use #FESM)

Reach Out and Connect With Someone

Many people think that pushing out content is the most important thing in social media. Not true. To really make social media work for you, you must also _connect_ with people every single day.

So, what exactly does it mean to make a connection? It simply means reaching out and making a friend with no ulterior motive, no other goal in mind other than to make a friend and build your network. What you want to do on social media is the one thing most people seem to miss, which is to remember to be social! You want people liking and commenting on your stuff, so you should also like and comment on other people's posts—yet don't forget to get in your prospecting activity as well. (We'll cover this in a bit.)

We recommend you set a goal to make a minimum of 10 "connections" per day. Yes, 10. The importance of this activity over time cannot be stressed enough.

Do you realize that connecting with 10 people a day is over 3,600 in a year? If you are brand new—starting with zero contacts—the process of connecting could grow your _network_ to thousands (no, the use of the word _network_ was not an accident).

This is network marketing, right?

Constantly be on the lookout for opportunities to be social and turn strangers—the "cold leads" that are everywhere around you on social media—into "warm contacts" by bringing them into your orbit, into your world.

The key is to get into the habit of reaching out and connecting with people every day—and at a minimum, every other day.

We kind of equate it to the gym. If your business goal is for you to grow your business, and you have a fitness goal of getting in better shape, well, it would be a good idea for you to get into the gym daily—or at least every other day.

Anything less than exercising every other day would not show much of a commitment to your health. Likewise, making connections with people on social media less than every other day would not be making much of a commitment to your business.

Prospecting on Social Media

As we discussed earlier in this book, there are two primary ways to build your network marketing business via social media.

The first way is social media marketing: the process of posting content on social media to provide value to others, which in turn allows you to make connections, build relationships, and draw people into your world. The second way is to focus on prospecting and recruiting. For purposes of review (from earlier in the book):

MARKETING is when you do something that you hope an unnamed individual reacts or responds to. It could be a status update, image, video, flyer, advertisement, billboard, etc. Marketing is passive where you hope someone takes action from it that notifies you in some way.

PROSPECTING is when you reach out to an

individual, online or offline, cold market (people you don't know) or warm market (friends and family members). It is YOU at least attempting to start a conversation with an individual.

A great analogy is the difference between farming and hunting. **Farming** is the process in which you plant seeds, water them, and wait for the crop to grow. **Hunting** is where you grab your coat, head into the woods, and find your next meal.

We're not suggesting that one is better than the other. We've used both to build our business. Both can be extremely effective. It's a matter of style and comfort. Some people are natural farmers and more comfortable with planting seeds and waiting for them to grow, which requires patience. Others would rather grab their bow and arrow and hunt.

We know people who have built large teams doing nothing but farming. We also know many people who have built large organizations without ever posting content, doing nothing but hunting for prospects.

In a perfect world, you do both.

Sadly, not enough people in network marketing are taking the time to learn how to prospect on social media and then actually do it. If you're one of the people who learns to do it and then truly does what you learned, you can literally dominate the marketplace.

What Exactly Should You Say?

No one can tell you exactly what to say, or how to say it. In other words, the words that come out of your mouth must be your own. They must feel natural coming off your lips—otherwise they will feel weird to you and sound "spammy" to the people you are trying to communicate with.

We all have a certain way that we talk to people, and people can tell even through social media if we're being inauthentic, especially now that you have audio messaging. People can tell that it's not really you, that you're trying to sound like someone else.

It's important, therefore, to come up with a formula that works for you. And in doing so, you'll have developed a process that will work for anybody on your team who wants to reach out to people, without telling them exactly what to say.

People see right through things that appear too polished, too canned...*too spammy.* They can tell it's a spam message and you're sending it to a million-other people. It's easier—and far more effective—when you are simply yourself.

Looking for Commonalities

When it comes time to reach out and connect with people, the absolute best strategy is to determine what you have in common with the person before making contact. As an example *(this is Jessica here)*: I play tennis, and so if I were prospecting and recruiting today, I might look for other tennis players to whom I can relate. I'd want to be able to "talk their language." I might dig deeper, too, and find out how many days a week they get to play tennis, how often they take off work to play if it's really their passion, and if they want to play more, why aren't they? It might have something to do with where they work or their current lifestyle.

Ray Higdon & Jessica Higdon

We had someone go through our training once who was a mountain biker, so he reached out to other mountain bikers on LinkedIn. Now he has a six-figure business. It shows the power of the connection and having something mutually in common with each other.

Once you start making friends and growing your network, make sure that you take the time to interact with people you're going to reach out to before you reach out to them. It will make the contact that much "warmer" than colder. For example, if you go into a Facebook Group, take the time to like, comment, and give value to people by sharing information or answering questions before you start reaching out.

Reaching Out to People

Let's say your target market is moms. So, one way of building your connections is finding someone you know that knows a lot of other moms. Maybe it's the leader of a PTA or something. It doesn't mean that you go and friend all of their friends in the next 20 minutes. For one thing, Facebook doesn't like that. Second, it's not going to be very effective.

I would look at the people connected to that person, in this case the different moms, and look on their profiles, look at their comments on people's posts, see who they are, and pick out something specific that stands out to you. All of those moms probably aren't a great fit for you, and you're not a great fit for them. Some might be super negative. Some might even have on their page something negative about network marketing. Don't waste your time with those people. Go for the people you feel are a good fit for you. Find something specific

PAGE 65

that really jumped out at you or, ideally, something you have in common and then reach out to them.

When it comes to reaching out to people, the "follow" button is your best friend, but I always ask people if I can follow them or if we can be friends first. Some people worry their message might not get into their inbox. If it's a mutual friend, then it might. If you have no connection to them whatsoever, then it might not—but that's when you get creative. If you send this person a message and it goes into their "Other" folder, then comment on one of his or her posts and say, *"Hey, by the way, I sent you a message, make sure to check your 'Other' folder, I would love to hear from you."*

Making First Contact

When you are ready to reach out, you want to make your first message enticing and friendly.

Start with a simple "Hey" with their first name in the first sentence, so that they know you're talking specifically to them and that this is not a mass message. Then, proceed to an enticing first sentence, followed by the reason you are messaging them. After that, have a connection point and a point of excitement. Then, finally, end with a question. (But do NOT send your link just yet!)

Why is it so important to have an enticing first sentence? Think of all the messages that come through your inbox every day. What do you immediately see as you're going through that inbox? It's the first sentence of the first message, right? That first sentence will be the main thing that determines whether you read it or not.

People prejudge all the messages they see based on that first sentence. If it says anything generic like, *"Hey, I see that we have mutual friends. Let's connect!"* (or something just as vague or impersonal), people will assume it is a mass message.

It's amazing how many people spend lots of personal time sending things that look like a mass message. That's just crazy.

An example of a great enticing first sentence would look like:

> *"Hey, Jess, I almost didn't reach out to you, but then I decided why not? I just didn't want you to think it was a spammy message."*

Call out the elephant in the room, using that as an enticing first sentence to get people to look at your message.

Also, when sending a message (this is a weird rule, but it works like crazy) do NOT send emojis and exclamation points. If you are using hype or cutesy techniques like emojis and exclamation points, you will lose 10% to 20% of people you could have recruited. Why? It takes away your personal power. You need to come across as someone who takes their business seriously and is a professional. And that's not sending emojis and exclamation points while prospecting.

The Four-Question Formula

Here are four questions you can use to lead people where you want them to go. You can use these questions over and over for every conversation, however, you must speak like a human being—don't just rapid-fire them off at someone. Don't make it sound like an interrogation. Have a conversation, be casual, and see where it flows.

1. *What do you do?*

2. *How long have you been doing that for?*

3. *You must love it, huh?*

4. *Have you ever considered doing anything else?*

"What do you do?" is a great first question. Then you can create the conversation using a logical flow. Focus on building rapport, then getting them where you want them to go. It looks something like this:

<u>You</u>: *So, what do you do?*

<u>Them</u>: *I'm in real estate.*

<u>You</u>: *Oh, that's awesome! How long have you been doing that for?*

<u>Them</u>: *About 10 years.*

<u>You</u>: *You must love it, huh? That must be so exciting.*

<u>Them</u>: *It pays the bills, right?*

<u>You</u>: *Well, geez, that doesn't sound like much fun. Have you ever considered doing anything else?*

That's where the conversation continues, and if he/she is open, you can introduce the person to a video or whatever the next step would be in your process.

For Products

When it comes to products, you may be going into Facebook groups or various fan pages and finding people with the problem you help solve, whether it is people with skin problems or trying to lose weight, or whatever. Such people present a great opportunity to share information about your products, however, the conversation goes a little differently.

First: a warning about the *wrong way* to reach out to someone about your products. Here it is:

Somebody is posting about trying "all this stuff" for some problem or issue. Then the network marketer reaches out to this person and says, *"Hey, I saw your post. You should try this."* Don't do that.

You can reach out, of course, but be a real person by connecting first. For example, start with a first sentence that shows you can relate—that you are paying attention. It could be something like, *"Hey, I saw your post. I can totally relate."*

Then ask a question. *"Do you mind sharing with me what you've tried in the past and why it didn't work for you?"* And then go from there and see if you can find an opening to mention your products. Find out about the person's history before you jump in and start sharing your products.

From there, you can say something like, *"Based on what you shared with me, I think you may want to take a look at what I do."* Or, *"I think you may have interest in this product. If you'd like to see some information, I can send it over to you, and if not, no big deal, but I think it'll really help."*

Remember to always give an "out" when prospecting. For

example, at the end, saying, *"It may or may not be a fit for you."*

It's that simple.

They may put you off and stall, telling you to reach out again later. If that happens, then simply check back with them later. Pushing too hard in the early stages of the conversation rarely ever yields the results you want. If they say yes, then go to the next step in your sales process.

The Power of "Posture"

A critical ingredient to your social media prospecting is what we call *"posture."* Posture is something we teach on a weekly basis inside our private community, Rank Makers, and it is, without a doubt, the most powerful ingredient to your prospecting success.

Posture is the belief in what you have and how you represent yourself to others, regardless of external acceptance or approval. This means that when a friend or family member tells you that your business is a scam or pyramid, you proceed on without crumbling like a cracker or getting defensive. We could write an entire book on posture, but here are a couple simple examples:

Prospect: *"These things don't work, why don't you just get something legit?"*

You, the "Postured" Person: *"Yeah, it's certainly not a fit for everyone. Well, let me know if you know anyone that does want to make some extra money. I've got to go meet up with someone right now, but good luck to you."*

<u>Prospect</u>: *"If it's network marketing, I don't want to have anything to do with it."*

<u>You, the "Postured" Person</u>: *"Cool, no problem. It is network marketing, and I love it, but it's certainly not for everyone. Hey, I've got to run, but best of luck to you!"*

Staying Out of Facebook Jail

A common thing we hear is that Facebook puts up a block when you're reaching out to too many people, commonly called, "Facebook jail."

Basically, it's when Facebook feels you are engaging in spamming tactics (among other things, but for the context of network marketing, mainly spamming), and it blocks your ability to comment, message, or in some cases, both. This happens when you copy and paste the same or extremely similar message to many people in a rapid way.

Follow what we teach in this book and you should not have this Facebook issue. Also, you can use Facebook Messenger to reach out to people as it doesn't have all the restrictions that regular Facebook does. Messenger also helps if you want to add more friends. As you add more friends and you get more mutual friends, Facebook allows you to connect with more people. You can also move to another platform like LinkedIn. Split your time between Facebook and LinkedIn or Facebook and another favorite platform if you want to hit your daily prospecting number.

Reactive Prospecting

In addition to proactively prospecting, the more content that you share, the more leads will come your way to whom you can reach out. Think of it as a form of *reactive prospecting*.

For example, if you see somebody on your Facebook Live who posts a nice, positive comment then you should take that opportunity to reach out to that person, and say something like:

> *"Hey. I saw your comment on my Facebook Live. Really appreciate it. And, by the way, you may or may not know this, but I have a business where I am constantly looking for cool people to work with. I don't know if I'm barking up the wrong tree. I don't know if you'd be open to it in any way, shape, or form, but if you are, I'd be more than happy to share it with you. And it may or may not be a fit for you. I have no idea."*

When you have a prospecting mindset, and you understand the right way to do it, your posts become a great way to find people and make a connection.

"If people would embrace getting on the phone with prospects quicker, they would get more sign-ups more quickly. Unfortunately, getting people on the phone has become something of a lost art."

-Ray & Jessica Higdon

#FESM

(Take a picture of this page and use #FESM)

Closing Doesn't Mean "Being Pushy"

At some point, you need to help people decide if they want to buy. At some point, you also need to help people decide if they'd like to join your team. In other words, you need to transition from conversation to conversion. That is, you need to close.

If you don't ask, you don't get—and all the time and effort at this point will have been wasted.

Some will say yes. Some will say no. There's no need to complicate it beyond that.

Unfortunately, a lot of people do complicate it. They associate "closing" with being pushy. For some people, even hearing or reading the word *closing* gives them a case of the hives. We get it. But don't worry.

When we say it's time to close, we aren't talking about being aggressive or pushy. We're not talking about forcing people into doing something against their best interest. All we're talking about is helping the person come to a decision.

Developing a Closing Mindset

First, it's important to understand that effective closing is all in the mindset you bring to the process.

There was a point in time where I *(this is Jessica)* was getting people to watch the presentation but once it was time to close, I wouldn't recruit any of them. I was having this disconnect, and it was so frustrating—if you've been there, I'm sure you can relate. I felt like a failure because I knew there was something I was doing wrong but didn't know what it was.

Then one day I caught myself.

I was sharing the presentation by sending people the video. Then afterwards, before I would even ask them what they liked about the video and go into the close, I found myself thinking, *"Uh, here we go again. They're going to absolutely hate it. It's going to be the worst. They're going to tell me it's a pyramid."* And I suddenly realized, by having that mentality, that's exactly what I was encouraging people to say to me!

It's strange but true: *Sometimes it's our own fear of something happening that creates that exact thing to happen.* How? When we have a *rejection mindset*, we keep telling ourselves things won't work out the way we want. And these negative thoughts impact our behaviors—including the way we speak, our words, and our body language—which impacts the way others respond to us. The very thing we're scared of happens because we made it happen with our mindset.

- *People who are overly conscious about money are the people who always seem to run into objections about money.*

- *People who are concerned about time being an issue are the people who always seem to run into objections about there not being enough time.*

- *People who are worried someone will challenge them about the business being a pyramid scheme are the ones who always seem to have people ask, "Is this one of those pyramid schemes?"*

We've been doing this a long time, and we can tell you this happens as a matter of fact—again, it's weird but true. Not every time, but more often than we realize, it is our fears and attitudes about things that influence outcomes more than the attitudes of the people we're dealing with.

If you have a fear of closing, you must change what you say to yourself right before you go into the close. The mantra for me *(this is Jessica still)* was: *They're going to absolutely love it.* Every time I would share the presentation and start to close, I would say to myself, *"They're going to absolutely love it. They're going to think this is the best thing ever, and we're going to walk away with at least a great conversation."*

As soon as I changed my thinking, there was an amazing shift in my results. Changing your mindset changes the way you think. Changing the way you think changes what you say—and perhaps, more importantly, the confidence with which you say it. And when you change how you come across, people can feel the difference in your confidence and your sense of certainty and conviction.

Moving the Close Forward

Once you have gone through the question formula and there's interest, you need to take the next step.

There are two things that will make or break the sale at this point:

1. If you fail to establish some other form of communication (for example, Skype, FaceTime, WhatsApp, or phone)

2. If you fail to set a specific appointment time for the person to look at what you have to offer.

Getting a Number

Once someone agrees to look at your information, say, *"Great! I'll text you the information."* If you want, you can even call out the elephant in the room which is, the concern someone might have giving you his or her number. So, you can add a P.S. of something like, *"By the way, I'm not going to be calling you constantly or spamming your phone or anything."* Few people have an issue giving you their number if you approach it this way.

Another way you can get a number is to send the information to them and then say, *"Hey, here's my phone number. By the way, what's yours, so I know who's calling me in case you have any questions?"* (News flash: They're not likely going to call you, so don't expect it.) Then, set up an appointment time to follow up with them as soon as possible.

If you want to stay on the phone with the person while they watch the video, that is up to you. But your goal should be to set an appointment time and then call them to follow up and close.

If you absolutely cannot get an appointment when you send the information, this is basically little more than throwing a *Hail Mary* (a reference to throwing a last-minute pass in American football). Doing so should be your fallback position, not your standard approach.

Follow Up and Close

When you follow up, we suggest asking a couple of simple questions. As always, feel free to change the exact wording so you feel comfortable saying it but try to stick as close to what we're suggesting as possible.

The first question is, *"What'd you like best?"* Or, *"What stood out to you the most? What'd you like?"* Then, from there, *"How do you see yourself building it?"*

If you are leading with the product, then your close would be asking a question like, *"How would having _____ benefit you, or feel?"*

And whatever answer they give, reinforce it. If they respond, "I actually want to do this on social media." Say, "Great, you can do that. In fact, we teach that." And then finally close by assuming the answer is yes. For example: *"Sounds to me like you're ready to join."* Or, *"Sounds to me like you're ready to get started."* Or, *"Sounds to me like you want to do this thing."* Then be silent. Because this is where a lot of people lose the sale, talking when they should be silent instead.

I'll never forget *(this is Jessica again)* one time on the phone when I finished my presentation and said, *"Well, it sounds to me like you're ready to get started,"* and the person didn't answer. He literally went quiet and said nothing for a full 20 seconds. This might not sound like a lot but holding your tongue for 20 seconds is like a lifetime—especially on the telephone. However, I knew better than to interrupt his thinking. Eventually, he broke the silence and said, *"Okay, let's do it,"* and signed up.

If I had broken the silence, I'd have also interrupted his decision-making process. And in the end, that's what we want—a decision. Yes or no, it is what it is, but the goal is to help people make decisions. Sometimes all you have to do to facilitate that is to just shut up.

We put an entire closing blueprint into one simple video that you can check out by going to CloseMorePeeps.com.

Do You Have to Get People on the Phone?

When it comes to selling people on your products or service, the answer is usually no—you don't have to get people on the phone. It can often be done online. But when it comes to presenting the opportunity? That's a different story.

We firmly believe that if people would embrace getting on the phone with prospects quicker, they'd have more sign-ups more quickly. Unfortunately, due in large part to the perceived ease of dealing with people online, getting people on the phone has become a lost art.

Don't get us wrong. Texting and audio messaging are great tools. Directing someone to a website to watch a video is a painless, seamless process. But, from our experience, you are at least three-times more likely to sign someone up if you can get that person on the phone.

We also understand that, in the end, people will do whatever feels most comfortable.

Leading With the Product Versus the Opportunity

For years, trainers have taught to lead with the business. However, then the FTC shuts them down and so it's like, "Well, maybe the product." Just know that percentage-wise, it is more duplicatable to lead with a product.

Why? Because the reality is, most people are not entrepreneurial minded. They're watching "Dancing with the Stars" and not "Shark Tank." Most people have a career or job, and they are not necessarily looking to change that. But everybody buys products. Everyone wants a new product that will solve a problem, whether it be nutrition, weight loss, or whatever.

Everyone likes buying a good product, and no matter who you are or what you do for a living, it's normal to share stories about your favorite products, things you've tried, etc. Then you add to that the reality that most people don't typically talk about making money.

We're not saying *not* to lead with opportunity, but if you haven't positioned yourself as an entrepreneurial person who is into making money, you should probably stick to leading with the product. And that's okay. Let other tools do the work of introducing the business. Nothing is wrong with this method, not to mention that leading with the product is always the most legally safe approach.

How to Re-Engage With Social Media "Ghosts"

One of the biggest questions we get around prospecting: *What do you do if you've been communicating with someone and then that person just disappears? How do you re-engage?*

The first thing to understand is that having people disappear is not unusual—so try not to over-react. Don't freak out.

The way to handle this situation is to start by asking yourself: *Why don't some people respond? What would make them respond?*

First, let's explore why some people don't respond. There are generally two reasons:

- They've been putting you off because they're busy.

- They've been putting you off because they don't want to join and avoiding you seems easier than telling you the truth.

In either case, pestering people with a bunch of messages asking, *"So, have you watched the video? Are you ready to buy? Are you ready to join?"* is not the answer.

Neither reason is a negative reflection of you, your product, your company, or the opportunity. They're simply busy. They're simply not interested. Neither is a big deal unless you make it one. So, at this point, the question becomes: *What would make them respond?*

The Fear of Missing Out

One of the most powerful forces in the world is what researchers refer to as FoMO—the Fear of Missing Out.

FoMO isn't just a cute catch-phrase—it's a real thing. It's a description of the apprehension and social anxiety people feel when they wonder, *"What are other people doing and involved in that I might be missing out on?"* FoMO also taps into the natural fear of regret we all have—that there will be a time in the future that we'll look back and regret what we didn't learn more about, do, or experience. This is especially true of events, investments, and business opportunities. And making bad decisions about all of the above.

Because of this, FoMO is one of the most powerful tools you have in terms of getting people to respond.

When it comes to attracting people to you—especially important, busy people—begging for attention and appearing desperate is not effective. You need to position yourself as someone who is equally busy, that you are moving and grooving, too. This makes you more attractive to other busy people, and it is very powerful.

Now, once a week, go to the people in your Facebook Messenger who haven't responded for four days or more and go through your contacts and say something like:

> *"Hey, I apologize. I have been so busy with new prospects and new customers and people that I totally dropped the ball in following up with you to see how you were. How are you doing?"*

Now, this may sound a little funny because *they're* the one that didn't respond. But, this message psychologically works. Why? Because when someone is busy—especially when someone is busy growing his or her business, not just watching cat videos—it's intriguing. It makes people curious. It makes them want to know, "What's so good over there? What is that person doing that's keeping him or her so busy?" In other words, what am I missing out on?

(Note: You must be careful here. You can't just copy and paste the same message over and over again, so don't go and do 100 of these in a row—if you do, you'll probably get blocked from Facebook for a period and find yourself spending time in Facebook jail.)

For the record: *"Just checking in"* is our least favorite follow up response. What it really says is, *"Just checking in because I need money and you haven't responded yet."* Don't ever *just "check in."*

How Long Should You Follow Up?

If you feel you've identified someone who would be a good addition to your team (especially if you think the person is a connector), don't give up on that person. Follow up forever. But do it correctly so as not to chase them away.

Two freakishly effective ways to reach out to someone you haven't talked to in over a month are updating and deflection.

- An *update* is a piece of information regarding something that's going on with you, your team, and/or your company, etc.

- A *deflection* is where you ask the person for a referral, so you are not going after the person directly, but indirectly.

You can do one or both. For example, here is a combination of updating and deflecting in one short communication:

"Finding people on social media who are local to you is simple, and it's a great way to build your business. When you learn how to build locally on social media, you can also teach your teams to do the same thing."

-Ray & Jessica Higdon

#FESM

(Take a picture of this page and use #FESM)

"Hey, I thought of you recently because our company is expanding into Great Britain, and the company is growing by leaps and bounds...it's kind of crazy right now. Listen, I don't know if this thing is a fit for you at all, but do you know anyone who may want to make some extra money, and may know someone in Great Britain as well?"

When you combine an update with a deflection, a lot of times people will reply, *"Wow, you guys are expanding into Great Britain, it must be going well,"* because you have provided information that has made them curious about what's going on in your business.

Don't Give Up on People Too Easily

It's important to not make yourself crazy over people who don't immediately respond. Often you will find they come back on their own, usually because they keep seeing your posts. If you're doing things right, people come back when they're ready, on their timetable, not yours. Focus on those who are interested or at least show some remote interest in having a conversation with you and taking the next step. This is not to say you give up.

We are big believers in what we jokingly call the "follow up until they pass away" plan—*only we're not joking*. We strongly believe you should never give up on someone entirely, even if you're only contacting that person every now and then.

The only reason to disqualify someone entirely is when the person is overly negative or nasty. We never want people like that on our team, and neither should you!

Warm Market Prospecting

When it comes to your warm market, meaning friends, family, acquaintances, etc., people often wonder what to say to them when using social media. It's very easy, and we have a process you can follow.

As with everything we suggest, remember you need to be natural. These people know you to some extent (in some cases very well), so don't feel like you can't be yourself. So, with that said, here is what we suggest.

First, reach out (assuming this is Facebook) and send a message with something simple like, *"Hey, it's been a long time."* Then wait for a response.

The reason you wait for a response is because you want to make sure that this person is still active on social media. You also want to make sure this contact has seen your message and that they know *you know* they saw your message. The ball is in their court to respond.

After they respond, you can say something like: *"Listen, I actually didn't reach out to you to chit-chat. I would love to catch up with you at some point, but..."*, then compliment them.

It's important to know that this is not a fake compliment. We're talking about something real and, ideally, the compliment would be about something that would make them a good fit for your business. For example:

- *"I remember you being a great networker..."*

- *"I remember you having a ton of friends..."*

Then, transition immediately to the business:

- *"I remember you being so outgoing and awesome, and you were one of the first people I thought of. I'm working on a project and would love to share it with you. Would you be open to a side project that wouldn't interfere with what you're currently doing?"*

As you can see, the last line above is similar to what we recommend in asking a "cold market" prospect. The big difference is how you start the conversation because this is not a total stranger. And, we also avoid making the mistake that most people make. What's that? Many people believe that when they reach out to a "warm market" person that they haven't talked to in a long time, they need to have an hour-long conversation about their entire life and then finally at the end say, *"By the way, I didn't even think of this, but do you want to get involved in my company?"* People will see right through that and realize that was the real reason you called them.

So, be upfront with the reason you are reaching out. It will save you and the person you are contacting a lot of time.

Building Locally on Social Media

Building a team locally on social media is awesome because it's like getting a bonus, or like getting two for the price of one. You get a recruit and, on top of that, they're close by. As such, sometimes you're able to duplicate them a little bit easier when that person is local to you.

Finding local people on social media is actually very simple and a great way to build your business. Why? Because when you learn how to build locally on social media, you can also teach your teams to do the same.

To be clear, it is not necessary to build locally first—or to focus on building a local business at all. It is possible to develop amazing connections with people who you have never met— and perhaps never will. That's one of the benefits of learning to use social media effectively. But, if you *do* have a desire to build locally and/or you find it easier to add people to your team by meeting them face to face, here's how it's done.

Using Facebook to Build Locally

At the time we are writing this, Facebook and LinkedIn are the best to build your business on a local basis due to their robust search functions.

From your Facebook profile, you can go to your friends list. When you pull up your friends, you'll see many different tabs (categories) at the top. From there you can either search for certain people or click on the current city you're living in, and it will show all of your current Facebook friends who live close to you.

If you've already reached out to some of these people, that's okay. There's no harm in going back to them and seeing if they have any openness to what you're doing. If you haven't reached out to these people, reach out to them.

The initial goal of reaching out to people is merely to see if you have something in common, some point of connection. For instance, maybe you have some mutual friends or know some of the same people local to you both. Figure out something you can connect with them on—and then mention that you live in their town.

Once you're connected, see if this person is open to learning more, offer to share the video presentation online, and then meet with him or her to seal the deal. You can also meet, show the presentation (if this person is a qualified prospect), and seal the deal that way.

Sourcing Locally

Now, you don't need to rely on just your friends and the local connections you have currently. Use a little creativity and you can find a ton of people local to you on Facebook.

For example, a great way to find and grow local connections is to visit local Facebook pages. For example, one of the towns near us is Naples, Florida, and the *Naples Daily News* has a fan page. There is also an upscale shopping center near us with a lot of different shops and restaurants called, Mercato Naples, which has a fan page—a fan page with tons of likes and a fair amount of interaction on the page. So, take some time and think of local places where people hang out near you and go visit those pages.

Think of local celebrities, too. Patrick Nolan is a local news anchor in our town with a fan page. See what we're saying here? There are an endless number of pages and groups for local people, places, and events with tons of interaction, people posting, commenting, etc. You just need to do a little digging.

Again, use your creativity and let these social media platforms do what they were meant to do: help you find and connect with like-minded people.

When it comes to LinkedIn, if you are already connected to someone, you can simply send that person a message directly. To build connections, like on Facebook, the process is the same. Search for people locally and then reach out to them. Simply find the "People" section within your profile and then filter them by different categories and keywords. Look for people with whom you have things in common, for example, same high school, college, workplace, and, obviously, the same city.

Say hello first and find a point of connection and common ground. Don't forget! Your goal here is not to go in guns-a-blazing, trying to recruit them. It's to make a connection—to make a friend first and *then* to see if they might be open to what you have to offer.

Meeting With Local Prospects

Here are a few considerations when it comes to meeting people you have connected with locally on social media:

- Only meet with people who have reviewed your materials in advance and have expressed some interest in learning more about the business—otherwise you're simply wasting your time.

- Maximize your time by setting up a "meeting day" so you can batch several meetings in a row, one after the other, ideally at the same location or somewhere very nearby.

- Don't spend more than 15 to 20 minutes at the first meeting. Doing this demonstrates you are busy and if you have scheduled your meetings properly, you truly are busy.

Finally, as soon as you sit down with the person, ask them if they liked what they saw and if they were ready to get started. Never assume the person isn't interested—always assume they *are*.

Handling "The Question"

So, what if they ask *the question*. You know the question we're talking about, right? What if they ask:

"Is this network marketing?"

The answer is to be honest and tell them: *"Yes, it's network marketing."*

This is what we have found to be the best approach, at least for us, because of one underlying and important factor. *It's the truth*. It *is* network marketing. And if you want to be freakishly effective on social media, the best place to start is by being truthful. Besides, the reason they're asking—with the assumed objection being that it's network marketing—isn't that it's network marketing.

The primary reason people get hung up is because of the way it's been shared over the years, with people going to such great lengths to hide it. That's what makes it sleazy!

We have found that the best approach is to ask questions that allow you to dig deeper. Questions like:

- *"Do you mind if I ask why you asked if it was network marketing?"*

- *"Did you have a bad experience of some kind?"*

You'll get all kinds of answers to these questions, and most of the time the person's answers will be what gives you the opportunity to deal with the underlying issue.

And sometimes you can't.

In any case, don't spend a lot of time worrying about getting the objection and definitely don't go out of your way to spend a lot of time trying to convince someone who is an absolute "no" to network marketing.

Setting Goals for Your Social Media Efforts

It should go without saying that it's important to set goals—not just in the world of network marketing but for any individual or business on the planet. This is also true when it comes to social media. And not just long-term goals but daily goals.

Why are daily goals important? Because consistency is the number one thing people struggle with when it comes to building their business. As such, we teach people to tackle small and doable activities every day to build their consistency muscle, rather than setting weekly or monthly goals.

Nothing is more daunting than starting the morning, looking at a monthly goal of reaching out to 150 people. It's far better to start the morning saying to yourself, *"I'm going to make this one call"* or *"I'm going to send out this one message,"* and then move on from there to the next and the next and the next. Small, doable goals win the day. Then, as your consistency muscle develops, you can expand to bigger goals, like five calls or messages per day. And then actually do it.

Focus on Activity, Not Results

People come onto social media sometimes and think that in the next two weeks they're going to get tons of people to sign-up. That rarely happens. Over time, yes, but certainly not right away. It just doesn't happen that quickly. Why? Think about it.

When you start on social media, your first task is to build a pipeline—a pipeline that then must be filled with strangers who are then turned into familiar acquaintances—and eventually friends.

It is not realistic to think you can jump onto a social media platform and create sign-ups instantly when you haven't sown the seeds of the relationship by providing value first.

It takes time.

The way to make the most of social media is to develop a mentality that says, *"I'm going to try to make as many friends as I possibly can by creating value, seeing if they're open to learning more about my products and/or the business, and if they are, great—and if they're not, that's okay, too."*

That's why your commitment to social media must be for a minimum of a year. You might see some short-term money come in, but, if you're reading this book, we're going to assume you're not after a few bucks of short-term change—you're after the big money, the big impact, and the big ranks in your company. And if you want to achieve that level of success, then you must make a long-term commitment. Don't be a social media dabbler—be a social media builder.

80% of Success is Showing Up

Woody Allen is quoted as saying that 80% of success is showing up. Whether this is true or not, and the exact percentage—70%, 80%, 90%—is up for debate. Let's just say that showing up is a critical element. Agreed?

Nowhere is this more-true than in the world of social media. But to be completely accurate, the saying should be:

*"80% of success in social media is showing up
again and again and again."*

One aspect of showing up is obvious, being that the more you show up, the more people you'll reach with your message and the more those people will remember you. It's the same reason why big companies spend tens of millions of dollars on radio, magazine, billboard, and television advertising. With the exception of infomercials that run in the middle of the night, most ads are not designed to get people to buy at that moment—only to create impressions and brand recognition in the minds of potential buyers for future purchases or for when they are ready to buy.

"Wishing to NOT have haters or doubters is a fruitless effort. If you want to make a big impact and build a business that means something to you, you will have haters and doubters. If you cave to them, the people you could have impacted will never get the help you could have offered."

-Ray & Jessica Higdon

#FESM

(Take a picture of this page and use #FESM)

It's the same thing on social media. The more that people see and hear from you, watching you care about them by delivering value with no immediate expectation of a financial return, the more likely they'll trust you when it comes time to invite them to do business with you.

Make no mistake, this takes time. You must be willing to show up for a long time...to own real estate in people's minds.

There's another, easily overlooked reason that showing up a lot is important: The more you show up, the better you get at showing up. The better you get at delivering value through your posts. The better you get at presenting concise nuggets of high-quality content that have true impact on others. In other words, showing up doesn't just improve the lives of the people you reach—you also improve your ability to help others.

It's a beautiful cycle.

What if You've Done It Wrong?

One of the questions we get asked is: *What if I've been on social media for a while and have done it all wrong—should I erase everything and start over?* The answer is no, you don't have to start over.

If you have been spamming your profile and wall with company pitches ("Join my Team pretty please!!") with links and other things that raises resistance and makes you look like a spammer, we suggest this: Delete all of your posts from the last 48 hours and anything that shows company or product names in your profile or cover photos. Then just move on. You don't have to start a new account.

If you posted and/or had conversations with people that you think may have offended someone—or perhaps you tried to pressure people unnecessarily—we suggest you apologize and have two powerful ways to do this.

First, you could do a Facebook Live that is vulnerable and says something like, "If you are watching this, I have an apology to make. When I got started with my home business, I was so excited that I vomited my company and product all over my social media, and many of you I reached out to with ineffective or pushy tactics and I just want to apologize. I am reading a new book that has really opened my eyes to how badly I was doing it, and I hope you can forgive me and help me on my journey of starting to add value instead of being salesy. Thank you so much!"

This is NOT an easy admission, but we have found that vulnerability is one of the most powerful weapons you can wield. The right people will forgive you and don't worry about the others.

The second way to apologize is by texting/emailing/private messaging those you feel you went overboard with. Something like, "Hey, I just want to apologize. I approached you about my home business in a really terrible way and I am learning new strategies of growing it but wanted to message you this apology. Hope you can forgive me and, if not, I understand."

The key is to do both of these things without an addiction to them being interested in your product or company. Don't go back and re-pitch the person you are apologizing to right away. You can re-approach them, but we suggest not doing that for at least a month or so.

This will go a long way to giving you a fresh start. Because you can't just pretend it never happened. It did.

Here's the good news: We can tell you that if somebody did offend us and then came back later and said, *"Some of the things I posted and/or said in the past were ridiculous and uncalled for, and I apologize to anyone I offended and hope you can forgive my behavior,"* well, not only would we forgive that person but they would probably become one of our favorite people on the planet because people just don't do that anymore.

Taking responsibility for your actions is an attractive trait. So, take responsibility and then let it go. There is no need to address it ever again. Anyone who sees your honest, heartfelt *mea culpa* and writes you off, well, you don't need them in your life/business anyway.

But I Don't Want to Be a "Guru"

Then don't.

The truth is there are a lot of people on social media who think that being a guru is what is required to attract people to them. Not only is it not necessary to present yourself as a guru, there are few things more off-putting than people pretending to be a guru when they're not.

Add to this category those people trying to act like their business is making a ton of money by taking selfies standing next to someone else's Ferrari.

This is a huge issue right now because everybody seems to be jockeying for position by putting on false fronts, when what people are hungry for is the exact opposite. They want honesty. They want authenticity. They want you just the way you are.

Presenting yourself for exactly who you are is the only sustainable model to follow.

Rather than pretending to be more than you are, why not just take people on your journey with you—from wherever you are to wherever you end up. That's the kind of person other people want to follow and be around.

If you can talk about the things you've learned, even if you only learned them five minutes ago—things that will help make other's lives better—they won't care when you learned it or how much money you're worth. They'll simply appreciate how you just helped them.

That's how you build a huge following.

Blogging as a Social Media Marketing Tool

Believe it or not, the term "blogging" just celebrated its twentieth birthday, having been coined for the first time in December 1997, but it feels like it's been around forever.

The question is, in the ever-changing world we live in today, how important is blogging to the success of your business?

The answer is a personal one.

Blogging is a marketing tool we personally use and have used for a long time, so we obviously think it's a good idea—*for us*. Does that automatically mean blogging is a good idea for you? Maybe.

First, it's got to be something you want to do. If it isn't, chances are good you'll quit before the results you want manifest. Essentially, all the effort you've expended will have been a total waste of time.

That said, there's a bigger problem with blogging. For many network marketers, blogging can easily become something they hide behind—something that creates the *illusion of connection* with people while being only that. *An illusion.*

Yes, people may be reading your blog, but are they truly connecting with you? Maybe, but maybe not.

Worse still, the illusion that blogging is helping you build connections often gets in the way of using social media to reach out to people. We've seen people put prospecting activities on hiatus because they're "working on their blog." Or they'll say, *"I just have to get this blog out there and then I can connect with people."*

That's a mistake.

If you want to grow a network marketing business, you have to be connecting and prospecting no matter what's going on, no matter what other activities you've got going. This goes for things other than blogging, too. Like writing a book, or doing a podcast, or creating videos for your YouTube channel, or whatever. Regardless of all the other things you're involved in doing, no matter how effective those things may be, you must not let those things keep you from your number-one activity, which is reaching out to people directly to see if they're open to your product, your service, and your opportunity on a near-daily basis.

Blogging is a good idea. Podcasting is a good idea. Posting

videos is a good idea. All of these activities can be good, unless you are using them as crutches or allowing them to become time-robbers that prevent you from reaching out to people. If you want our training on Blogging and Marketing, register for the next one at AttractPerfectPeople.com.

Why It's Important to Build an Email List

The obvious reason for building an email list is it allows you to communicate with people who have shown an interest in what you have to offer, or, better still, people with whom you've developed a personal relationship.

But there's another, just as compelling reason only few people ever think about. And that reason is ownership. *Yes, ownership.*

What we're about to say is not designed to scare you, though it is a bit scary. And that is the fact that you do not own your Facebook page, nor do you own any of your social media accounts. Anything you've ever signed up for, for free, is not yours—you do not own it. We do not own our Facebook pages, nor do we own our Facebook profiles, and neither do you.

Here's a bad story, but it's a story people need to hear.

I *(this is Ray, now)* have a friend who flew me to Manchester, England, to speak to his team several years ago.

My friend is a top earner in his company and had done all of his prospecting on Facebook. Then he got hacked. The hacker got into his account and started changing things and causing all kinds havoc. As a result, his account was shut down. He never got it back, and he had to start over from absolute scratch. And I have my own horror story to tell.

At one point I had 22,000 subscribers to my YouTube channel, and one day—poof! All gone. What's worse is, I hadn't taken the time to find ways to connect with my subscribers via email. When the channel was pulled (too long a story to go into here), there was no button to push that would allow me to say, *"Hey guys, my account was shut down!"*

The account was gone.

Your email list is different in that you do typically have some ownership over it. It's the free stuff that'll get you into trouble. If you want to try out the email service we suggest for network marketers, check out RayHigdon.com/aweber.

You're No One Till Somebody Trolls You

One of the things that plagues people who spend time on social media is dealing with the negative, mean, and sometimes downright nasty things people say.

First, you must understand that internet/social media "trolls" are out there, and everyone must learn to deal with them. *Everyone*. You are not alone. But consider this: if you *aren't* getting negative comments, then you're probably not playing big enough! If you play even slightly large in the world of social media, you are going to attract some haters—you simply are.

When our students or clients get their first hater, we tell them to celebrate it by saying, *"Hey, I got my first hater!"* It means they're starting to play big.

This is Ray again: I had haters and doubters when I left a high-paying corporate job to get into real estate. These naysayers told me it would never work out. And when I started network marketing? I had haters and doubters, too. They told me I was an idiot.

I had haters and doubters when I was the number-one earner in a network marketing company and offering successful training courses. I still get haters even now that we have trainings but are no longer building a team. If I catered to all the haters and doubters, I just would not be in business. Wishing to NOT have haters or doubters is a fruitless effort.

It's also important to remember that people who feel the need to drop negative comments on social media are not happy with the state of their own lives—it's not you they hate, they hate themselves. People who are happy with their lives simply don't waste their time attacking other people—they've got better things to do.

Dealing With Negative Comments

The short answer is, don't. Just ignore them. Now, for the longer answer.

Depending on the severity of the comment, there may be times where you feel compelled to respond, if for no other reason than to let it go. Most of the time, when we get someone who is really slamming us for any reason—real, in their own minds, or imagined—we'll say something like, *"Hey, sorry this just didn't resonate with you, and we wish you the very best."*

Don't be part of the problem, be part of the solution. Putting more anger into the universe is never the answer. Retaliation is for losers. Think karma. Besides, the last thing any of us should want to do is attack someone who is already suffering from a lack of self-esteem. The person who is lashing out at you is living a life filled with fear and pain. Be the bigger person and don't add to that, even if you're justified in doing so.

We can tell you from personal experience, we've always regretted the times where we didn't use our better judgement and allowed ourselves to get into long, drawn out battles with people. Doing so will only take you off your game. Protect your mental energy.

Using Contests and Giveaways

If your goal is to create contacts and conversations, contests and giveaways can create excitement and buzz, but we've never found them to be effective when it comes to converting strangers into customers and team members.

There is also the issue with everything you do being duplicatable. You need to always be asking yourself, *"Can the average person do this?"* If you're giving away something small, then the answer is probably yes. But if you're giving away $5,000 worth of stuff, the average person is not going to be able to do that. Giving away one unit, of whatever it might happen to be, is not only duplicatable, but it's smart.

It's Not Too Late to Start

Have you ever looked at all the people out there on social media and thought, *"Well, should I even do anything because there's already all these people doing it?"*

Maybe you think the people you see being successful on social media had an edge. A leg up. You might believe they came onto the social media scene with big teams already. Many people think that way. They think that if everyone is doing it, it must be oversaturated—it's too crowded, so they don't do anything.

By the same logic, no one should ever write a new book because there are so many books already. But there are always new books being written. Why? Because there is always room for new ideas—or old ideas shared by someone new, in a fresh and different way.

Admittedly, social media is still a little like the "wild west," and we are all learning as we go. But people are still people. There will always be things that come up you are not prepared for. Guess what? The only way you get good at handling those challenges is to experience them, and then learn what works and what doesn't. Don't let the "what-ifs" keep you from building a network marketing business on social media. You can choose to get started and create something amazing for yourself and help others do the same. The choice is yours.

Is Social Media the Future of Network Marketing?

In a word, yes. Social media is indeed the future of network marketing.

Over the last few years, we've encountered many leaders in the profession—big leaders with enormous teams—who were not big believers in social media, people who said social media would never work. They said it wouldn't work because it would never duplicate. Now, many of these same people are admitting that social media is *the* place to build a business.

Does this mean it's impossible to build a robust business without social media? No, of course not. Belly-to-belly networking still works, and it always will—but it's not the number-one thing that people will be doing in the future. To think that your business can grow as fast without social media is to ignore the reality of the world in which we live today. Simply put, social media can help you reach out to so many people so much faster.

So, yes, the future of network marketing is social media—and you do not want to get left behind.

If You're a Leader...

If you're a leader, you must come to the realization (if you haven't already) that even if *you* prefer not to engage in social media, most of the people who join your team in the future *are* going to want to use social media to build their business. And if you don't know how to use social media as a team-building tool, how can you teach it? Not understanding and mastering social media is a big detriment to you and others. After all, if you can't teach them how to use it, they may just go and find a leader who can. Also, if you're someone who has generated over $100,000 in your network marketing career, be sure to ask about our Network Marketing Alliance, which is a free association for leaders.

Social Media Versus Live Events

Does this mean social media is a replacement for events, large opportunity meetings, and company conferences? Probably not. But we're already seeing the impact on attendance at company events due to people asking themselves, *"Why do I need to go to the company event? I'm connected to everyone in our Facebook group!"*

This is short-sighted, of course. There's no question that people have major breakthroughs at events that could never have been achieved from behind their keyboard.

Patience, Persistence, and "Pumping the Well"

Want to be successful on social media? Be patient, persistent, and keep pumping the well. Because marketing is a marathon, not a sprint. If you're going to be involved in social media, you need to be in it for the long haul, where you are putting out content and building connections every single day.

Then, one day, you will see things happen. The key thing is to keep filling your pipeline with connections. And eventually—if you stick with the process—you will one day have a sudden influx of activity and wonder: *What was the one thing I did that made it happen?* The answer will be that it wasn't *one thing*. It will be the cumulative result of *everything* you've done.

The Urge to "Throw-In the Social Media Towel"

Before you consider abandoning your social media efforts because you're not seeing results yet, we encourage you to ask yourself: *What's the alternative?* What's the alternative if you don't develop the patience to continue?

And when you're feeling restless, wondering if you're wasting your time, consider this: *Quitting is selfish.*

Quitting keeps your stories, your content, and your valuable information from others who need it. On the other hand, if you don't think about quitting every now and then, you're probably not trying hard enough. Quitting will not speed up your progress at becoming freakishly effective at using social media.

Finally, let's be honest: Engaging people on social media isn't all that hard to do. Not hard like cracking rocks with a sledgehammer in the hot sun or digging ditches. So, what if it takes five years to achieve your goals? Five years is going to come and go whether you're actively building your social media presence or not, so you might as well just stick with it.

At a very minimum, give yourself the gift of a full year of activity, building your social media presence by reaching out to people, growing your network, and sowing seeds. If you give yourself at least one year, we can almost guarantee you'll start seeing tangible results.

Even better, why not embrace the one word that literally guarantees your success—the word, "until." Do it until...

Until it works.

Until people start to notice and respond.

Until you get results and reach your goals and dreams.

Until you help change the lives of those around you.

Until...

Until...

Until...

You Want to Succeed.
We're Here to Help.

The Higdon Group is passionate about helping network marketers reach their highest potential by equipping them at every level with the knowledge to succeed.

Creating and sharing content with global audiences striving for and achieving results, the Higdon Group is truly a unique company set apart in the world of network marketing.

The Higdon Group stands apart from others by always giving back to their members, followers and live-event attendees with generous amounts of content and programs to keep up with the ever-changing industry of network marketing.

To learn more about how to recruit on social media, register for our next training at http://RayHigdon.com/jess

To learn how to better recruit cold market prospects, register here: http://rayhigdon.com/coldmarket

To learn how to implement online marketing to grow your network marketing team, register here: AttractPerfectPeople.com

---

Want Us to Blow Your Audience's Mind?

For information about having Ray and/or Jessica speak at your next event, email our team at: support@RayHigdon.com

---

What is Rank Makers?

Rank Makers is a worldwide community dedicated to becoming the highest producing group inside the network marketing profession.

How are we doing this?

By creating an incredible community of like-minded people and by working with you every single day. This community is our priority. That means every single day, inside the community, we are coaching and training you on some aspect of growing your business, then following up with a simple action step you can take to get results.

The results we are getting are fantastic, and the community is thriving and growing bigger by the day.

To learn more about becoming one of the new breed of network marketing superstars, visit:

https://joinrankmakers.com

TESTIMONIALS:

"Thanks to the social media training I have received from Jessica & Ray, I have become more comfortable with conversations without awkwardness, connecting with new people on a regular basis, Rank Advanced in my company after trying for 15 months, and today I just received my largest company paycheck, which puts me on track to replace my day job income this year."

- Lenise Whitfield

"Within one month of me joining Rank Makers, I slammed through a top rank in my company. After one week of my team member joining, she crushed through two ranks, and within three hours of another team member joining, she got her first customer ever! One week, another team member has lists and lists of leads and prospects interested in the business. And these are just the ones that stand out for me recently! My whole team is joining Rank Makers, and I want to encourage you all to NOT keep this group a secret! Share it! The amount of content and training is priceless. I am beyond grateful that I can grow my business and know my team is getting REAL and RAW training that works and can duplicate. Just wanted to share."

- Marina Simone

"Thanks to the social media training I received from Ray and Jess, I have been able to recruit 67 new reps, enroll 23 new customers, and rank advance to the highest rank in my company! I had recruited a few before but NEVER like this!"

- Trip Knowles

"My first two weeks in Rank Makers I prospected 43 people, recruited two people, and rank advanced."

- Lisa Romanovitch McManus

"My commission has increased by tenfold! I've never made this much before and am very close to hitting a huge rank."

- Holly Lucas-Gallup

"After seeing the social media training from Ray and Jess, I have been able to double my recruits every single month. What's more important is that I was so able to teach this duplicatable way to my team, which is seeing results as well!"

- Richard Valkovic

For more testimonials, visit:
www.IsRankMakersLegit.com

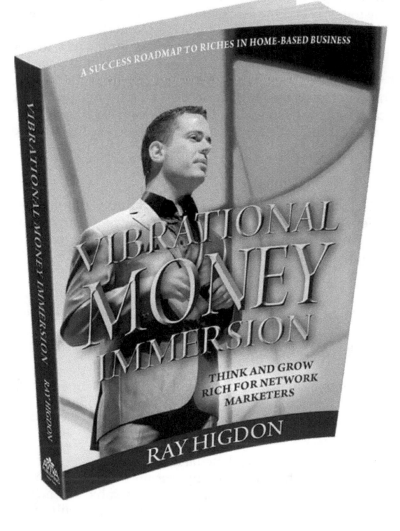

Available at: RayHigdon.com/vmibook

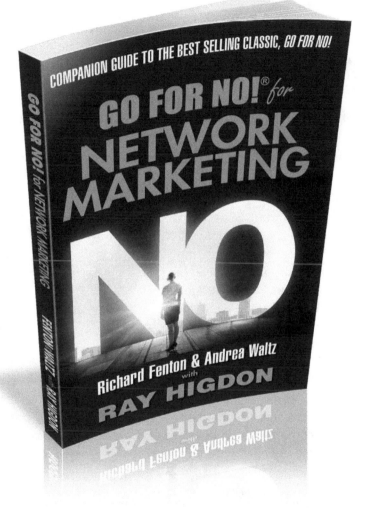

The #1 Amazon Network Marketing Bestseller!
Available in Kindle, print and audio at Amazon.com

About the Authors...

Ray Higdon is a two-time best-selling author and a former number-one income earner in a network marketing company he joined while he was in foreclosure. He has shared the stage with Tony Robbins, Bob Proctor, Les Brown, Robert Kiyosaki and many more. Ray and his wife no longer build a network marketing company so they can better serve the profession as coaches, speakers, and trainers. Ray blogs almost daily on www.RayHigdon.com and is the co-owner of the Higdon Group.

Jessica Higdon started in network marketing when she was only 21 years old. Because of her age and lack of connections, she had a very small warm market. After striking out with friends and family—and not signing up anyone in the business for the first five months—she turned to social media. Over the next 18-month period, Jessica built a six-figure residual income, using mainly Facebook, and became the number-

one female income earner in her company. Since then, Jessica has created multiple training programs that have grossed over one million dollars.

Together, Ray & Jessica's coaching company, The Higdon Group, was recognized on the Inc. 5,000 as one of America's fastest growing companies, and they love helping network marketers grow large teams and create freedom in their life.

CPSIA information can be obtained
at www.ICGtesting.com
Printed in the USA
LVHW05s1606051018
592522LV00002B/2/P